"Absolutely riveting. This fast-paced, immersive book reads like a novel and tells the truth of one family's legacy of faith and love through displacements and wars, across decades and continents. A must read for anyone who loves a great story and is interested in learning about the complexities of a region often misrepresented in the West."

— **Jessica Goudeau,** author of *We Were Illegal: Uncovering a Texas Family's Mythmaking and Migration* and *After the Last Border: Two Families and the Story of Refuge in America*

"Vividly empathetic, Leyla K. King brings her family's tale of survival to life, sharing a direct, clear-eyed account of her grandmother's displacement from Palestine. At this memoir's urgent heart is a celebration of strength and resilience, resonant with a love of language. It follows King's foremothers across decades and nations as they reckon with the exigencies of dispossession and the circumstances of their identity as Palestinian Christians. All who owe their existence to a journey will find something to love in these intricately braided sagas."

— **Sarah Cypher,** author of *The Skin and Its Girl*

"Leyla King's *Daughters of Palestine* is a poignant and fascinating multigenerational tale of a family's flight from Palestine to the United States. Taking the reader from the village of Shafa 'Amr in 1920s British Palestine to Houston, Texas, in the present day, with stops in Haifa, Beirut, Damascus, and other Middle Eastern cities, the book weaves together family stories of love, hope, and faith. Set against the backdrop of exile and displacement, these tales demonstrate the power of family and faith to help people overcome tragedy. This book is a must read for anyone who wants to understand the experience of Palestinian Christians, who are often overlooked in discussions of the Arab-Israeli conflict."

— **Nicholas E. Roberts,** author of *Islam Under the Palestine Mandate*

"*Daughters of Palestine* is a glorious celebration of Palestinian motherhood, sisterhood, and daughterhood. Leyla King's writing sings as she narrates the multigenerational epic of her Palestinian Christian family. Chronicling her family's loves and losses from Haifa to Beirut to Damascus to Houston, her beautiful book is testimony to the power of connection, of faith, of home, and above all, of story. An essential book for our times."

— **Stephanie Saldaña,** author of *What We Remember Will Be Saved: A Story of Refugees and the Things They Carry*

DAUGHTERS of PALESTINE

A MEMOIR IN FIVE GENERATIONS

LEYLA K. KING

William B. Eerdmans Publishing Company
Grand Rapids, Michigan

Wm. B. Eerdmans Publishing Co.
2006 44th Street SE, Grand Rapids, MI 49508
www.eerdmans.com

© 2025 Leyla K. King
All rights reserved
Published 2025

Book design by Lydia Hall

Printed in the United States of America

31 30 29 28 27 26 25   1 2 3 4 5 6 7

ISBN 978-0-8028-8499-2

Library of Congress Cataloging-in-Publication Data

A catalog record for this book is available from the Library of Congress.

For Grandma, of course

and for Dad

A NOTE TO THE READER

These are the stories of my ancestors — and they are my stories, too. They are tales handed down from one generation to the next. With one exception, I have not changed names and have tried, as best I can, to pass these stories on to you as I received them. Everything in these pages is true to the best of my knowledge, but as in the telling of any good tale, I have taken the storyteller's liberty to imagine dialogue, color in less-vivid scenes, and provide plausible details in empty spaces.

This book tells the story of many through the eyes of three women:

Aniiseh, my great-grandmother, daughter of Za'leh and Amiin, wife of Wadii', mother of Bahi,
Bahi, my grandmother, daughter of Aniiseh and Wadii', wife of Fariid, mother of May,
and me, **Leyla**, daughter of May and Joe, wife of Ben, mother of Beatrice.

You will see one of our names at the beginning of most chapters to indicate who is speaking. Each of us has our own story to tell in our own voice. And in between our stories, you will find the stories of our places and our people.

My grandmothers and I don't stand alone. Our stories often intersect with the personal histories of other people, are born from another tale's end, or break open to reveal yet another story nestled within. So, interwoven between and among the generational line that connects me with my grandmothers are other tales that we share, like modern-day Scheherazades, so that you can better see and know us through the ones who have peopled our lives, through all the ones whom we have loved and who have loved us in return.

And so it begins, dear reader, with my grandmother Bahi who turns my attention — turns our attention — to the mothers who came before her and the daughters who have come after.

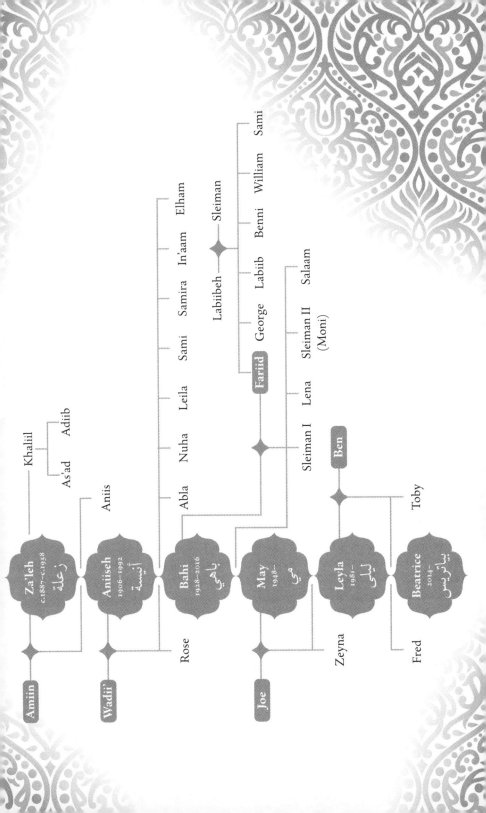

BAHI · THE SHINING ONE

Houston, 2002

We start with laughing now.

This granddaughter of mine. She sits in front of me, her light brown hair tucked behind her ears and hanging down below her shoulders, her green eyes — *my* green eyes — in her father's Irish face looking back at me. She presses "record" on the little cassette tape recorder, and we look at each other and we laugh.

"We start with laughing now," I say.

Months ago, in her final weeks of college, she called me and asked to do this together. Of course, I said yes. "It would be my pleasure," I told her. But it's so much more than a pleasure, really. It is right that we should do it together, she and I. It is meet and right so to do. This is what the priest says on Sundays when we share communion. This is a kind of communion, too. And it is meet and right that she should be the keeper of my stories.

Since I was a small child, I have been a listener and a learner. And a retainer. I read books and newspapers and the Holy Scriptures. I listened to the newscasters on the radio, to my mother's gossip with our neighbors, to the men's card-table conversations as I served them coffee. I have retained it all. And now I am old. I don't think I am losing my ability to retain it, to keep it safe in my heart

1

and in my mind, but you never know what age will steal from you. And I will not live forever. Better to pass the stories on, to let her keep them, to retain them, for whoever comes after me. My legacy, passed down from generation to generation, like the blankets I knit for my grandchildren, like the intricately painted plates that I serve hummus on to my guests.

She is so fair, so light. She is my whitest grandchild. Of all eight of them, she and her sister are the only ones who don't call me "Teta." But I love the way the word "Grandma" rests on her tongue. And in the end, what does it matter, the language we use to communicate, so long as we address each other, call to each other with the names of love. Grandma, she calls me. And I call her "habiibti," "Leylati," the child of my heart, the keeper of my stories.

As a name, "Leyla" evokes the beauty of a dark night. It's ironic, really, then, that she should be so fair, so light-skinned: *el-shaqraa'*, the fair one, my mother — *allah yerhamha* (may she rest in peace) — called Leyla when she first held her great-grandchild. Later, when she was a toddler, Leyla would stand before my mother and they would talk to one another — Mama speaking only Arabic, having lost her grasp of other languages in her old age and Leyla understanding only her native English. But they were enamored of each other, nonetheless. Mama, I know, was taken by her fair-skinned great-granddaughter. And Leyla? What do we know of a child's mind? Perhaps, even then, even over differences of language and culture, she was collecting the stories, retaining their power in her small body to grow within her even as she grew.

And grow she did, into this girl — this young woman, sitting before me, tentatively rolling her *r*'s and tasting the majestic *Daad* of the Arabic language now and then as we talk, still in English, but with a seasoning of the Arabic that she has worked so hard to begin to gather to herself. She repeats the names of the towns and villages I tell her about to make sure she gets them right: Haifa, Beirut, Damashq, Shafa 'Amr. And she spends minutes forming the names of her ancestors on her tongue just so: Aniiseh, Wadii', Amiin, Za'leh.

Yes, Za'leh.

We start with laughing now. Now, in the comfort of my own home, with steaming cups of tea before us and the promise of the cookies I made yesterday awaiting us in the kitchen, we share these stories, to be recorded and retained and remembered, with joy and thankfulness. But it wasn't always that way. There was much suffering, too. To get to this place, this moment, with Leylati, there was first pain and heartache and so much loss. And grief. And upset. Yes, upset and sorrow. *Za'leh.* We start with laughing now, but before that, first, there was Za'leh.

SORROW
A STORY

In those days, the whole region was ruled by the Ottoman Empire, the Turks. And it was called "Greater Syria." But it was not very great. They were all poor. Everyone lived in poverty. Even the rulers themselves. They were a poor empire at that time, declining quickly. Everyone knew hunger and illness.

Their village, not far from Haifa, was called Shafa 'Amr. It means "the healing of 'Amr." The legend says that the great hero of the Muslim expansion in the Middle East experienced severe stomach problems until he drank the waters of this place and was cured. And so the people named their village to remember the miracle.

But the people were never only Muslim. Until the *nakba*, they always lived together as happily as people ever do. We are, after all, the same people. We were neighbors and friends. Together, we celebrated each other's weddings. Together, we mourned — the whole village mourned — when death came to make its claim among us. We held each other's joy and grief because we all shared the same experiences, with the same traditions and foods and music and dances. The same culture, the same language, the same God: Muslims and Jews, the Orthodox and the Druze, the Maronites and Protestants and Catholics. Different but the same; we didn't fight or exclude.

Well, not generally. Za'leh *was* excluded, though, by her brothers-in-law and their wives. Because they were Protestants —

Anglicans — and Za'leh was the fourth daughter (and therefore called "sorrow" or "upset" because her parents expected a boy) of a Catholic family, who married the third 'Asfour brother, Amiin. And they liked their neighbors of other faiths, but when it came to marrying, it was looked down upon. *She* was looked down upon. The Protestants considered themselves superior to other faiths. It was silly, really. We know better now, but in those days. . . .

In those days, the Anglican girls went to missionary schools and were taught to read and write, but not Za'leh. And so her sisters-in-law despised her because she was Catholic and illiterate — and because she was beautiful. Olive-skinned with green eyes. By far, the prettiest of the wives of the three 'Asfour brothers, but unloved by all except her husband.

They lived together — all of them — in one home. Each family had one room in the apartment on the upper floors above the warehouse where the 'Asfour brothers, grain merchants, negotiated deals and sold their wares. Even after the children came, Za'leh lived in the small compartments of her husband's home.

But children did come. Beautiful children. Very good-looking, like their mother. Aniiseh first. And then her brother, Aniis. They did it that way then. The daughter named the feminine characteristic, the son the masculine. It means "the sociable one." Perhaps it was Za'leh's way of combatting her own loneliness and isolation, of bearing forth her hopes for a different future where she would be welcomed and cherished.

If so, it was futile. Not long after the birth of her children, the world erupted in war and everyone was affected — even the 'Asfour family, tucked away in Shafa 'Amr. Amiin and one of his brothers were conscripted into the Ottoman army. They didn't want to go. Who would? Even the Turkish soldiers were malnourished and badly clothed, their horses unfed. Foot soldiers of the Ottoman Empire, drafted into a fight they had no interest in, Amiin and his brother, all the Arabs, were treated even worse than the horses. Mere months after the brothers' departure, the family received word that they had both been killed.

Za'leh had thought her children would bring her security, if not love, from the 'Asfours. She had, at least, borne the required male child, a son, to the extended family. But they didn't even give her space to mourn her husband's death. She had barely enough time to put on the black dress and the black lace veil of mourning before they kicked her out of the home, that clothing the only thing she carried with her.

The children they kept. It would be a pity for such beautiful children to be raised by an illiterate Catholic, they said. So they confiscated the sociable ones from her, cut her off from them, and sent her away, empty and desolate.

She had no choice but to return to her own family. But not for long. It wasn't seemly for a woman of a marriageable age to be alone, and she had held on to her beauty, even through the years of loneliness, childbearing, and grief.

And so they married her off again, this time to the wealthy herdsman, Khaliil. He had acres of land and hundreds of sheep. She lived in his mansion on the land he owned, benefited from the kind of luxury she had never known in the small rooms of the 'Asfour home, with housekeepers, servants, and a cook to do the work. She was free to worship as she wished, and she bore two more boys: As'ad and Adiib. But Khaliil was old, and she did not love him and never would.

Za'leh. The curse of her name followed her still. Sorrow and upset trailed her, as close as her shadow, tied to her feet wherever she went.

As soon as they were married, Khaliil's flocks started dying. One after another, over the course of months and then years, the sheep died, the workers left, the servants deserted the home, and Za'leh was left to pick up the pieces with two young children under her feet and an elderly husband always in front of her face.

She loved As'ad and Adiib, but she longed for her older children, too. For Aniiseh and Aniis, the sociable ones, the stolen ones.

The years passed in sorrow and a slow decline. Then, finally, her boys became young men who might aid and support her. Like their older siblings, As'ad and Adiib were beautiful; they inherited her olive skin and green eyes and their father's strong hands and wiliness. They were well-liked in the village and confided in their mother their hopes for a brighter future.

As'ad had just celebrated his eighteenth birthday when the fever began. His complaints of an aching head and an upset stomach grew worse. As his fever climbed, he scraped at the sheets of his bed, the cough bending his body over double. He drank little and ate nothing at all. Three weeks later, he was dead.

Once again, Za'leh had little time to mourn such loss, for already fourteen-year-old Adiib had caught the typhoid fever from his brother. Her younger boy survived — but barely. The illness affected his spinal cord, and he would never walk properly again. Za'leh spent the remainder of her life bringing her last child, the only one left to her, from one doctor to another, hoping to straighten that which had been made crooked, to make upright what had been bent by the changes and chances of life.

ANIISEH · THE SOCIABLE ONE

Shafa 'Amr, 1920

In those days, we thought the British were angels. It's no surprise, really. All our lives, in the missionary schools, in the Western greeting cards and magazines, even in the Christmas cards we sent each other, manufactured overseas, angels were always so light. They weren't just bathed in light: they were light-skinned, white as the feathers of their wings. Only the evil one, *Shaytan*, was dark brown or black, with curly black hair like ours.

When the British arrived in Shafa 'Amr after the war, whether wearing their red soldiers' coats or their white nurses' uniforms or their smart teachers' belted skirts and blouses or the buttoned-up suits of the businessmen, they all bore the fair hair and eyes of their Western island, and we thought they were angels. We welcomed them into the village with the lulus of celebration, as we would for the bride and bridegroom at a wedding, as Jesus was welcomed into Jerusalem, with palms waving.

And in a way, the British acted like angels, too. For in them was a kind of salvation for us, a drastic and desired departure from the backward tyranny of the Turks who came before them. We may still be a conquered people, a country ruled by ones not of our own race, but at least these rulers brought much to help us. They opened clinics, hospitals, and schools. They taught our mothers about cleanliness and good hygiene so that infant and maternal mortality declined. They brought antibiotics and technologies and wealth like we had never seen. They opened doors to a world we never would have known without them.

They were not all bad, the British. Indeed, at the time, we thought they were heaven-sent. Now, of course, looking back, I can see it was so much more complicated. *They* were so much more complicated. But then again, aren't we all?

At any rate, bad or good or somewhere in between, the fact is that they came. And we welcomed them. And if the missionary teachers insisted we speak English (though they taught us to read and write in both languages), if the nurses tsk-tsked at our mothers for their old wives' wisdom, if our fathers' bosses spoke to them sometimes like children, it was a small price to pay — a slight nod of tacit assent to our own inferiority in order to gain the superior wealth of our rulers.

And as for my brother Aniis and me — we whispered together, beyond our aunties' ears, outside even the confidences of our beloved cousins, wondering what this new day would mean for us, made orphans by both the war and our family's hardness of heart. Perhaps the white Anglican missionaries would insist that we be reunited with our mother. Perhaps our uncle would be convinced by the enlightened British that we belonged with the woman who bore us.

They were idle hopes, in the end. After her expulsion from our father's home, we never saw her again as children. I, at least, had clear memories of her. I was almost eight when she left. Aniis was barely three. It was left to me to remind him of her love for us — a love he remembered only in snippets: the smell of hot lemon-water she drank every morning and evening, still on her lips when she kissed us awake or to sleep; the clink of the gold bracelets, our father's wedding gift to her, as she stroked his cheek; the whispered prayer to the Holy Mother that Aniis could recite, even years later, young as he was when she taught it to him.

But the British would never have known all of that. Now I see that they probably couldn't even distinguish me and Aniis from our cousins. In their eyes, we were just the 'Asfour children — if they knew our name at all — dark-skinned and numerous. Even the priest was unconcerned about the longings of our hearts.

Our lives did change, though, after the British arrived. Almost immediately, Aniis and I were split up for the first time. I dreaded leaving my little brother behind, but I couldn't help being excited about what lay ahead. Along with my cousin Liina, three months older than me, I was being sent to the boarding school in Nazareth. The walls of Uncle's house had long felt too close for me; schooling from the British would offer the expansion of my mind, if nothing else.

Uncle walked me and Liina to the edge of the road to meet the wagon, the collar of my dress still wet with Aniis's tears, my aunties' admonishments still ringing in my ears. They called it the American wagon in those days, an invention from so far away having finally made it to us. It was a simple wooden open-topped box, rectangular in shape with four large spoked wheels, pulled by two horses at the front. Liina and I climbed on along with other passengers — mostly grown but a handful of schoolchildren like us — to make the twelve-mile trek to Nazareth.

We would come back home from school only twice each year — once during the Christmas vacations and again at Easter. Our family was too poor to pay the wagon's fare otherwise. I didn't mind, though. I didn't like school that much, and I missed Aniis dearly. But he had been sent to the Friends School for Boys in Ramallah the year after my own departure, and my uncle almost never paid to have him brought home to Shafa 'Amr. Plus, I minded school less than I did Uncle's stern looks and cold demeanor or my aunties' constant nagging.

In the end, though, I thank God for my aunties, unloving as they seemed to me. They were first cousins themselves, both of them from the Habiibi family. So when Wadii' Habiibi needed a bride, his mother was told to contact the cousins in Shafa 'Amr. "They have two eligible girls of age," the family reminded her. "One is the orphan — she's not much of a catch. But the other will be given a dowry. Ask for her hand."

And so that Easter, when Liina and I were home for the holiday, Wadii' took time away from his work in Egypt to come with his mother and father, from Haifa to Shafa 'Amr, to sit in the pews three rows in front of us and in the opposite aisle, to sing the alleluias, and to catch a glimpse of the 'Asfour girls — Liina and me — through the dark lace of our veils.

After the service, his father spoke in deep tones to Uncle, but Wadii' pulled his mother aside and whispered to her: "That girl, there," he said. "That's the one I want. The one who hides behind the others." For, despite my name, I was always shyer than Liina, whose boldness sometimes shocked me.

"No no," his mother replied. "That's the orphan, Aniiseh. She is the poor one. She has no father and no mother. Her uncle does not care for her. She comes with only the clothes on her back. It is the other one, Liina, that we want for you."

But Wadii' was insistent; he would not accept his mother's pleas or hear his father's advice. Before they returned to Haifa he would be betrothed to me.

That very afternoon, they visited our home. As they settled themselves on the settees, Liina and I prepared coffee in the kitchen, poured it in the silver pot and bickered over which of us would take in the tray. She won. But it didn't matter. The parents fell silent when she passed the coffee around anyway.

Half an hour later, the guests left, and Uncle called me into the sala.

"Wadii' Habiibi is a good man," he told me. "He has a good job in Egypt, and his father is the son of your aunties' cousin in Haifa. He has asked for your hand in marriage, and we have accepted. You will not find a better match, should you be fool enough to wait for another one."

I kept my eyes downcast, looking at the gold brocade against the dark background of Uncle's house slippers that peeked out beneath his trousers. Of course, I wouldn't have argued even if I was unhappy with the match, but, on the contrary, I was ecstatic. To leave my uncle's house, a place that had ceased to feel like home to me since my mother's expulsion, to leave the drudgery of school, to leave the small worlds of Shafa 'Amr and Nazareth, and all to enter adulthood with the attractive man whom I had snatched glimpses of today.

He hadn't seemed much taller than me, but he was handsome, with short sideburns and a crop of curly black hair on the top of his head. Beneath thick eyebrows, his eyes were small, because, for the most part, he seemed always to be smiling, which pushed his full cheeks upward toward his eyes. His wide grin revealed rows of straight teeth that shimmered against the dark mustache on his upper lip. And his broad shoulders seemed to me an assurance of his strength.

But I couldn't dwell too long on the picture of my betrothed that I had brought to mind. My attention was drawn back by the sound of my auntie's voice admonishing me. "Don't you dare mention it at school," she was saying.

So my escape was not to be as imminent as I imagined. If the teachers at my boarding school discovered I was engaged, I would be expelled. They didn't want the girls gossiping about boys and the intrigues of an adult life and sharing information that was unfit for young girls' ears. So I was to keep the engagement a secret until the term ended and I could finish out the year.

But I had a few days left yet to savor my newly acquired status of betrothed before boarding the American wagon back to school. And in that time, I looked forward to meetings with Wadii' and his family.

The very next morning, they arrived at our apartment with a beautifully carved wooden box, inlaid with glistening pearl, and presented it to me as I sat on the settee. I lifted the lid to find the first gifts of my engagement: silver and gold bracelets, rings and necklaces with precious stones, and the single gold band that symbolized our betrothal. I slipped it over my finger — a perfect fit.

Over the next few days, Wadii' and I sipped endless cups of tea and coffee together under the watchful eye of his parents and my aunties, the adults exchanging pleasantries on the other side of the sala. It was not enough time to know him, but I had the whole of my life to discover the nuances of his personality, so I was not concerned. He seemed affable, kind, and generous, contrast enough to my austere uncle.

And then one morning, my aunt demanded the gold band from me and tucked it away in her apron. "You'll get it as soon as the term ends and you return for your wedding," she assured me. "Finish your schooling first."

And so Liina and I walked with my uncle to the side of the road where we awaited the American wagon; it was all so usual, so prosaic, and yet it felt to me entirely *changed*, as though the landscape were brand new, the faces of the people on the wagon aglow with an energy I'd never seen before, the bumpy, dusty road beckoning to an unknown future even though I knew it just led to Nazareth and school. But now, *now* I was engaged. Only six more weeks of lessons, and then I would be free of the demands of childhood.

Except I didn't make it nearly that long.

On the first full day of school, all of the students gathered for the opening assembly. We filed into the open courtyard and awaited the arrival of the headmistress. Liina stood on my left, keeper of my secret. When I turned to my right, I discovered Selma next to me. I knew Selma and liked her. We had been classmates for a number of years. A pretty girl, plump with a round face and an easy smile. More outgoing than me, she was a better friend to Liina, but we got along well. Nonetheless, I was surprised to see her sidle up to me for the morning assembly. I soon found out why.

"You've been engaged to Wadii' Habiibi, right?" she whispered gleefully.

"Shhhhh!" I responded harshly. "How do you know that? It's a secret. No one is supposed to know. I'll be expelled."

She giggled, her right hand covering her full lips as she tittered behind it. Simultaneously, she extended her left hand out to me, showing off a thin gold band. "I'm engaged to his next younger brother! He asked for my hand over the holidays, and my family accepted!"

I turned to face her and couldn't help but reflect her enormous grin back at her. She was obviously as excited as I was — and clearly less able to keep a secret. Before I could stop her (*would* I have stopped her if I could?) she leaned over to the girl on her other side and whispered something in her ear. I couldn't hear the words, but I could imagine them: "Aniiseh and I are engaged to the Habiibi brothers! We're going to be married soon!"

And that was all it took. Before the day was ended, Selma and I found ourselves in the straight-backed chairs of the headmistress's rooms. "Ladies, there are rumors that you are betrothed? Is this correct?" she asked us, the crisp consonants and broad vowels of her English accent leaving no room for half-truths. Selma grinned; I blushed. We both nodded.

We were permitted to spend the night at the school, in a small closet of a room separate from the other students, but the next morning, I clambered back up the wheels of the American wagon and settled myself in for the bumpy journey home to Shafa 'Amr.

I suppose the headmistress had wired my uncle in advance to tell him of my expulsion, because he was waiting at the side of the road to receive me. We walked home in silence. Was he angry? Annoyed? Unmoved? He was as inscrutable to me as ever. My anxiety grew with each step. What reception awaited me at home?

My worry was unnecessary. My aunties shrugged off the early expulsion from school; they knew Selma from their shared connections in Haifa — the whole of that family could never keep a secret anyway. And my return to Shafa 'Amr meant that I could help my aunts better prepare for the upcoming wedding.

How I longed for my mother, though, hungry for the love and support that she might have provided. My father's family offered the basics for the ceremony, and Wadii' had already promised to shower me with anything and everything I might need for my trousseau, but none of them could replace the special bond a mother has with her daughter during her engagement.

I wrote to her often in those final days of my girlhood. And I was permitted to read her letters back to me. I knew that she had remarried, that her husband was old, that his wealth was dwindling, that she was still pessimistic about life, always dreading the future, but that she was not unhappy. And I knew that I had a baby brother, newly arrived in my mother's home away from me. Even as I held no hope of meeting him, I wondered about him. I wondered, too, whether he might soon have a nephew of his own, young as he was. I wondered about the process of conceiving his nephew — or niece, I supposed, but hopefully nephew. I wondered about my wedding night with Wadii' and longed again for a mother to whom I could ask such questions. For not even my aunties would do in this case. "*'Ayb!*" they would cry at me. "Shame! Shame that a girl should be asking such things," they would say. But I could not write these questions to my mother, and there was no one else to ask.

She sent me the most beautiful headdress, though. She had stitched it herself, the fine filaments of red thread on a white background of high-quality cloth. The edges were patterned with rectangular blocks of geometric shapes in different hues — from almost pink to dark rust. And the center boasted carefully placed flowers, intricately embroidered, no two alike, but all of the same bouquet. Interspaced along one side were gold coins for luck, attached, I knew, by her own hand with tiny knots of the thread. She would not be there on my wedding day, but I could feel her love for me, nonetheless, sewn into every strand of the headdress, and I treasured it.

So I spent the weeks before my wedding writing to Mama and sewing what I could for my own trousseau and receiving Wadii' when he could make time to visit me.

Automobiles were rare in those days still, but Wadii' had a bicycle. With our wedding day so close, he had not gone back to his work with the Palestine Railways in Egypt but remained with his family in Haifa. Most days, he would bike the fifteen miles from the city to Shafa 'Amr, arriving at my uncle's house hot and tired and thirsty. When I heard his knock, I looked out the window of the room I shared with Liina when she was home, and I could see him in the street below.

I could hear, too, Uncle's booming voice through the door: "Who is it?" Of course, he knew who was at the door. Who else could it be in the middle of the day, knocking at the door that led to the apartment above my uncle's warehouse? But Uncle had always taken pleasure in wielding what little power he held, whenever he could.

And Wadii' would call back through the door: "It is me, Wadii' Habiibi, *ya 'amu*. I have come to see Aniiseh, to see my bride."

I never knew what my uncle's answer would be. There never seemed to be a pattern to his permission or refusal. Some days he would let Wadii' in; more often he would turn him away. He'd say, "Why do you insist on bothering us? What do you want with a young girl like Aniiseh? *RuH!* Go away." No amount of logic ("But she is my betrothed, *ya 'amu!*") or pleading ("I have come all the way from Haifa to see her!") would change his mind. And I would watch Wadii' climb back on his bicycle and pedal off down the dusty road.

When he was allowed in to see me, I would rush to prepare a tray for him — a large glass of water, a pot of tea, some cookies and dates to feed him — and carry it into the sala. We would sit together, across the coffee table, under my uncle's eye as he pored over the ledgers for the warehouse at the other end of the room. As he reached for the sugar, Wadii' would wink at me and smile and whisper, mostly jokingly, "When I marry you, I'm going to kill that uncle of yours."

We were married in the morning of Ascension Day. I was fifteen years old. Wadii' was a young man of twenty-five. We left the church under a shower of petals and the lulus of the village women. Liina grabbed my hand and squeezed it as I passed her by. My brother, home for the occasion from his boarding school in Ramallah, smiled shyly at the edge of the gathered party. I let go of Wadii's hand, pushed through the crowd to Aniis and hugged him to my chest. For a moment, I thought it might be impossible to let him go again. It felt like such a huge departure, a leave-taking that would fill me with unbearable grief, to separate myself from him, like losing my own name. Aniis. My little brother. The friend of my heart. When would I see him again?

We traveled immediately to Haifa and spent the night at Wadii's family's home. And the next morning, we boarded the train to Qantarra, on the east bank of the Suez, where we would begin our life together. Among our things was the leather trunk filled with my trousseau — dresses and underclothes, tablecloths and napkins, linens and soft cotton towels — all of the finest quality, all of them purchased by Wadii' for me, as he had promised, excepting only the headdress my mother had sent, which I had stowed safely near the bottom of the trunk, wrapped in paper to protect it from the dirt and dust of travel.

Forced into orphanhood by my father's family, I had been an alien in my own home throughout my childhood, as though I never belonged, not truly. But the minister's words at the altar, binding me to Wadii', had worked like some mystical magic transforming me utterly, from orphan to wife, from alien to queen. Now I was going to Egypt on the train, with *jowzii*, my husband (the word still felt intoxicatingly new — in either language), among all the many other passengers, but I felt as though I was as important as the English ladies who sometimes visited the village, with their expensive dresses and white parasols, nodding and smiling at us as we gaped at them. Now I was like one of them, as finely dressed, as prim and proper. Now when the other passengers looked at me, they would see a young woman, not a girl. A young woman with her husband, traveling to her home. A grown-up. An adult.

Wadii' worked in an office job in the engineering department of the Palestine Railways Company. It was a government position, and it was very well paid. He earned more than enough to have his own family and still send money home to his parents to supplement the good income his father made as a schoolteacher in Haifa. I had married well indeed. The Habiibi clan were among the wealthiest and most well educated in the whole city. And I was their eldest son's wife. I blessed my mother for the good looks I had inherited from her even as I said a prayer to ward off the evil eye that was sure to accompany such fortune.

The accommodations that were provided to us by the railroad company were excellent: spacious rooms with cool tile floors, large balconies overlooking the picturesque streets, even house servants that cared for the property. There was little for me to do, so I set myself to the task of welcoming Wadii's friends and associates into our home even as they came to welcome me as his new bride.

Wadii's boss and his wife were among the first we entertained. I had settled into the house, unpacked my belongings and was eager to prove myself as a worthy mistress of the home. I directed the servants to prepare a banquet for Wadii's boss — all of the traditional dishes of my people. *Ma'lubeh* with lamb, stuffed grape leaves and zucchini, hummus and *baba ghanoush*, *tabbouleh*, warm, freshly baked pita bread.

They arrived early — the British always did — but I was ready for them, nonetheless. The coffee table in the sala was spread with olives and cheeses, fresh radishes, thinly sliced, and small cups of arak, white as the couple's skin. We toasted to new beginnings. And I was so proud of myself, of my clear English — just as good as Wadii's — of my beautiful things, of the lovely home of which I was mistress. I should not have been so proud. Such pride is of the evil one; it should have been no surprise that it would be sorely punished.

Dinner ended; we had retired to the settees in the living room with cups of dark, sweetened coffee. The boss's wife had expressed her admiration for us — for me, I imagined — for much of the evening. The decorations of our home, my dress, the food, our conversation. I preened in her favor. As our guests began to collect themselves to leave, Wadii' insisted that they part with a gift from our home — a reminder of our hospitality and friendship. I nodded enthusiastically as he stepped from my side into the hall toward the inner rooms. It was right that they should have some token of our respect — one of the many brightly colored scarves we had brought with us from Haifa to give away to friends in just this kind of situation or even one of the light blankets we had received as wedding gifts from cousins.

But when Wadii' returned a few minutes later, he carried a long, white cloth embroidered with various shades of red, the gold coins along one edge jangling together. Before I could even speak (how could I have spoken anyway and dare to refuse to give the gift my husband had chosen for his English boss?), he smiled in his charming way and poured my mother's headdress into the wife's open arms, like a libation. The woman marveled over it, examining its intricate details and exclaiming over its beauty. "Thank you," she said. And then tried it in Arabic: "*shukran*." As though even she realized that a gift so precious required a response in its own mother tongue.

I plastered a smile on my face, my cheeks hurting with the effort, my eyes smarting with the pain of holding back my tears. When Wadii' closed the door behind them, he turned to me, beaming, I knew, over the success of the evening. But he was met by my anguish.

"What? What is it? *Habiibti*, what's wrong? *Ya Allah!* What has happened?!" he asked, distraught.

And I cried out to him, "The headdress! My mother's headdress! Why did you give that, of all the things we have, to that woman?! Why would you deprive me of my most treasured possession from the mother I have longed for for so long?!"

He looked at me in disbelief. "Oh Aniiseh, *habiibti*, I am sorry," he said. "I only wanted something for her that she would recognize as being something unique, something beautiful, something *falastinii*, Palestinian from our own home. I just opened the wardrobe and found it and brought it to her. And look — I was right — she will not forget us."

"I have nothing else," I moaned. "Nothing from Mama, nothing from Aniis. Your boss's wife will never forget us, but what do I have to remind me of the ones by whom I am loved who are so far from me?"

"*Ma'alesh, habiibti, ma'alesh*," he comforted me. "You have no need of these things, for I love you. I cannot bring back the headdress; I cannot restore your mother to you. But I can take you to see your brother. The Christmas holidays are not that far away. We will go to Ramallah, and you will see your brother. We will go together to see Aniis."

THE LOSS
A STORY

In those days, women got pregnant when they were very young. They spent their whole lives child-getting and childbearing and child-rearing. And of all the children a woman bore, she was lucky if three or four of them survived.

Aniiseh did not see Aniis that Christmas. By the time the holiday drew near, her cycle, which had only begun a few years earlier, stopped entirely. She was pregnant. Wadii', despite the difference in age and experience from his wife, was just as excited as she was. Their first child. He was convinced it would be a little girl. She knew it was a boy. Both of them could picture the baby already in their mind's eye, though the pregnancy was so young.

Wadii' decided that it was risky for Aniiseh to travel too much given her condition. The couple would return home to Haifa to spend the holiday with his family, as was right, but an additional trip to Ramallah to see Aniiseh's brother was impossible. But in the early days of Advent, Aniiseh's pestering began. She worried so about Aniis; his letters were sparse and breezy, as one would expect from an eleven-year-old boy. Still, Aniiseh knew herself how easy it was to feel homesick at a boarding school — even if "home" was a place you never really had.

Wadii' could never resist Aniiseh's requests. He had loved her from the moment he saw her in the pews in Shafa 'Amr, and he had made it a kind of game in his own mind to tease out, as often as possible, that shy smile from the downcast lips of his beautiful but wounded bride. So when she pressed him now, over and over again, to go to her brother, he was caught between the competing goods: to please his beloved wife or to care for the new life she carried.

In the end, he decided to do both. "It is not good for you to travel to Ramallah unnecessarily," he told her. "But let's go home to Haifa. I will leave you in the care of my mother and my sisters, and I will go to see Aniis, to make sure he is well and to bring him your love and comfort." He didn't get her smile, but she agreed. And they boarded the train to Haifa together.

Though it was Christmastime, the 'Asfour family could not or would not take on the expenditure of bringing Aniis home to Shafa 'Amr, so he remained in his school in Ramallah. Wadii' was always suspicious of the 'Asfours' claims of poverty when it came to Aniiseh and her brother. After the short train ride from Haifa to Ramallah, Wadii' walked the remaining miles to the Friends School for Boys. The early afternoon air was bitterly cold, and he hugged his coat around him, tucking his gloved hands underneath his arms for extra warmth. As he walked, the first large flakes of snow fell before him and he watched them land, uncertain whether to cling to one another or melt away. By the time he reached the school, the snow had begun to accumulate in white patches along the road.

Wadii' paused in the drive outside the main building of the school and looked up. The Quakers were well known and beloved missionaries. Despite the austerity of their tradition, these Quakers, all Americans, had a kind of ease about them, an openness and friendliness that the more buttoned-up British lacked in their relations with the native populations of Palestine. But as Wadii' glanced up at the blank windows and quiet shell of the school building before him, he got no sense of warmth. Of course, with all of the students and most of the staff away for the Christmas vacations, there would not be much activity expected. But surely Aniis wasn't sitting alone in one of those cold, empty rooms of the school?

He couldn't quite draw up the courage to knock on the large front door to be answered by the hollowness that he knew must lay within, so he looked about him some more. He noticed a soft light in a ground-floor window in the corner of the building to the left of the school's main entrance. Comforted, he made his way toward that door.

An old woman answered his knock, and when he stated his name and the name of his charge, she opened the door wider to let him in. Aniis was sitting in front of the large fire that took up one wall of the kitchen he had walked into. Wadii' had been right: students and staff had all gone to their homes for the Christmas holiday. The only ones left were Aniis and the cook — an old Arab woman who had long served in her role for the school. The two of them — ancient and youth — were keeping each other company through the dark days of winter, tucked in front of the fire that was their only source of warmth.

"Aniis, my brother," Wadii' called out to him as he sat gazing into the fire before him. "*Kul 'aam wa inteh bikhayr!* Merry Christmas!"

When Aniis turned to him in surprise, the same smile that Wadii' spent so much energy trying to make appear on Aniiseh's face burst easily onto her brother's visage. Aniis sprang from his chair and held out his arms to Wadii'. As he bent slightly to embrace his young brother-in-law and kiss his cheeks, Wadii' noticed how pale Aniis was, how thin and tattered his clothing. But Aniis must have inherited all the optimism for his family — which would explain Aniiseh's persistent pessimism — because the boy made no complaints about his situation. He seemed hardly to notice the cold and was unaffected by the prospect of spending Christmas with the old woman in the quiet kitchen of his school. Rather, he met Wadii' with joy, expressed gratitude for the unexpected visit, and asked after his sister with interest.

But Wadii' knew that, if he left his brother-in-law like this, he could not return to Haifa and report to Aniiseh her brother's circumstances and expect anything like Aniis's smile to appear. So he postponed his trip back to Haifa and traveled to Jerusalem instead. He bought warm clothes, good food that would last for days, and a few special treats for Aniis and brought them to him at the school. He wondered at the 'Asfours' lack of concern for one of their own, but at least he could go home to Aniiseh and tell her truthfully, and with a clear conscience, that Aniis was well cared for and happy.

He felt satisfied as he relaxed in his seat on the train ride back to Haifa. He had done his duty to Aniis; his wife was in his family's home, where she would be treated well and loved; and he himself had worked hard to provide her with a life of comfort into which they would soon welcome their own child. Christmas Eve was only a few days away and Wadii' looked forward to it with gratitude. *I thank God for all these blessings*, he thought, *for God's providence is assured.*

He walked to his family's home from the train station, whistling the tune of one of his favorite Christmas hymns, smiling to those he passed on the street. But he fell silent as soon as he opened the door, for he was met not with the bustling sounds of his mother and sisters in the kitchen, shooing his father away, but with a low, keening wail from the hall. He set down his case and walked briskly toward the back bedrooms. He found his mother and sisters there, bustling indeed, but not with the work of preparation for the Christmas feast. They hovered around Aniiseh, and she lay supine on the bed, moaning and crying.

"*Allah ynijiina!* God save us! What's the matter?" he asked breathlessly. The women — all except Aniiseh, whose eyes remained closed over her tears — looked up at him in surprise; they had not heard him enter. For a moment, the only sound to be heard was Aniiseh's soft wails, like the wind whistling through empty streets. Finally, his mother spoke to him tenderly, delivering the blow as softly as she could: "*Ya ibnii*, she is bleeding. The baby is gone."

He could feel the color drain from his face. Gently, he pushed his sisters aside, placed his hand on Aniiseh's dark hair in unspoken sympathy, and then left the room, closing the door behind him.

It was a somber Christmas that they celebrated together. Even as they welcomed the baby Jesus into their midst, they couldn't help but mourn the first baby of the next generation that was not yet to be. And Aniiseh never left her bed, the hum of her grief clanging discordantly beneath all their hymns of nativity.

Wadii' had to be back in Qantarra before the new year, but Aniiseh was in no state to make the long journey by train. So he left her there to be ministered to by his mother in mourning as she had been in the first blush of expectant joy.

Whether due to her grief or to the physical responses to the body's loss, Aniiseh became ill. For the first few days after Wadii's departure, her fever ran high and she would call out alternately for her husband and her mother, both of whom were far from her. In time, she began to recuperate, and her in-laws took seriously their responsibility to care for her health.

Finally, two weeks into the new year, she was well enough to be sent back to her husband in Egypt. Her father-in-law escorted her to the train station. They walked together into the trainmaster's office.

"Here is my son Wadii' Habiibi's wife," he told the trainmaster. "I trust you will ensure she makes it home to her husband in Qantarra safely."

The trainmaster looked upon Aniiseh and frowned. "No, Uncle," he replied. "I'm sure you must be mistaken. I know Mr. Habiibi well, and I know his wife. She is young and beautiful and of fine stature, but the wind would carry this girl away."

Aniiseh let her father-in-law speak for her: "She has been ill and unwell, *ya ustaadh*," he said. "But she is much better now. Let her go to her husband and take comfort in his strength. All praise be to God."

So she boarded the train, and Wadii' met her at the station in Qantarra. And she drank cod liver oil daily. And she improved in health.

ANIISEH · THE SOCIABLE ONE

Qantarra, 1926

In those days, I was still young. Too young, perhaps. Youth is resilient, unlike old age. When I became old, every bone of my body creaked with every movement. Every step must be taken with care, for a fall might be fatal. But the bodies of the young, we think, are indestructible, capable of anything. But maybe it's not so. Maybe the growth of new life demands too much of the young body. One must be fully formed oneself to form another within. And I was only fifteen when I lost my first child.

When I returned to Qantarra from my husband's family in Haifa, Wadii' met me at the train station. "I hardly recognize you," he told me. And though there are some who might be ashamed to admit it, my husband waited on me after my return. These things were not done in that time. The man is not meant to serve his wife. But Wadii' loved me in that way, nonetheless. I wonder whether I ever returned his love with the same fervor?

And perhaps my youth did make recovery — at least physical recovery — easier. A few months after the loss of my first child, I fell pregnant again. I prayed to God to see this new life through its earliest stages. I feared seeing or feeling the bleeding that had alerted me to the loss before. But first week after week and then month after month went by. My confidence grew with my belly. All would be well. I stopped praying for God's protection.

The child had quickened in my belly, and I had been carrying him — I *knew* it would be a boy — for six months. We would not travel so far as Haifa again, but I was far enough along in the pregnancy that the early dangers seemed well past. So we took our vacation by the seaside, not far from our home. It was there, strolling beside the gentle waves, that I felt the first pains.

Initially, I didn't recognize them for what they were. But the reality of what was happening quickly became clear; the tightening of my womb sent not-so-gentle waves throughout my whole body. And with the pain came the fear: surely it was too soon.

I was right. It was far, far too soon.

They delivered me in the hospital. Not just the son I so desired but a daughter, too. I saw them both, briefly, before they were whisked away among whispers of the evil eye. Such tiny and translucent bodies, as though made from my own tears.

Remember, I was only sixteen.

Of course, I wasn't the only one. Even with the modern medicines that the missionaries brought, in those days, so many children died. It's a miracle, when you think about it, that any of us makes it to the point of birth. So many things can go wrong as we are knit together in the darkness of our mothers' wombs. So many moments when the whole project of life hangs by a thread. Is it any wonder that so many pregnancies are lost? The wonder is that so many lead to the birth of a child — healthy and whole and holy.

No, I was not the only one among the women of my time to lose so many children, but it still affected me. When my twins died before they knew this life, my tears began and they never seemed to stop. Like Elijah's pot, the well of my tears never dried up. Even when my womb filled again and again, I carried that emptiness with me, low down and heavy in my heart.

But my womb did fill again — only a few months later. If I could have held my breath for all those forty weeks, I would have. Instead, I began praying the moment I discovered the pregnancy and never stopped. Please, God, let this one live. Please, God, let me bear a son into the world.

And the Lord answered my prayer — the first one at least.

As the end of my time drew near, when we knew that the child would live, Wadii' began whispering to me at night as we readied ourselves for bed: "She will be the most beautiful little girl," he said.

And I would tut at him: "*Laa' laa' ya jowzii.* No, my husband. Pray God we bring a boy."

"No, I don't want a boy," he said. "I want a girl. A daughter as beautiful as you are. And I will buy expensive ribbons and tie the largest bow atop her head." And he grinned at me. And I couldn't help but smile.

She was born in August. She was not the boy I longed for, but she was my child, my first living child. She was delivered of me loud and most definitely alive. And I rejoiced in that. She was precious to me, my daughter.

Had she been a boy, we would have named him Shukrii, after Wadii's father, as is our custom. But by the time my son was born, Wadii's brother had long since taken that name for his own family. As it was, with our girl, we decided to name her after Wadii's mother instead. But Wardeh was such an old-fashioned name, the name of an old woman, not a young girl, not a black-haired, black-eyed baby that enters the world proclaiming her own vitality. So we used the English translation that seemed to fit her better, and we named her Rose.

In those days, a woman spent forty days recuperating from the trials of delivery — she and her newborn babe cocooning together, learning how to be, how to relate to one another, mother and child. And Wadii' spared no expense on my recovery. He brought home nutritious meats and luscious fruits and sun-ripened vegetables. And the servants cooked the foods and fed them to me. And I fed Rose and fended off, as best I could, the dark thoughts that gnawed at the edges of my mind, the depression that threatened my soul even in the freshness of the new and vibrant life I nurtured from my own body.

When the forty days were over, the friends and neighbors, Wadii's colleagues and acquaintances began to come. Wadii' held a big party for our friends. The bottles of arak were opened, and the men toasted over the head of my baby as the women sang joyful lulus of celebration. And Wadii' took the baby from me and held her in his arms and stared into her face and told them all, "This is my girl. *Bintii*. Rose." And I knew she would grow up spoiled by him.

I did not spoil her — but I loved her. In the early months, I breathed in her scent, changeable as it was. Sometimes rank, sometimes sweet, sometimes familiar as my own, but always warm and alive.

Motherhood did not come naturally to me, though. In many ways, I was still a child myself. Despite the servants, I struggled to negotiate the baby's needs along with the responsibilities of the household and my own unpredictable emotions. Every time I looked at Rose, I couldn't help but be reminded of the ones who had come before, whose eyes had not opened into this world, and I grieved them. But Rose grew and flourished in her first year of life. And then I fell pregnant again.

My correspondence with my mother, still living near the village of Shafa 'Amr with her husband, had continued throughout my married life. I confided in her my fears and joys and sorrows. I knew she had two little ones of her own now — my halfbrothers. As'ad, the eldest, was nearly five, and Adiib was almost exactly Rose's age.

I pleaded with my mother to come to visit me. *Bring my brothers*, I wrote to her. *Help me in my new motherhood, and aid me as I prepare to welcome a son of my own. I feel so alone.*

And she agreed.

It was all quickly arranged. Her husband would put her and the children on the train, and my husband would meet them at the station in Qantarra. They would stay until my new baby arrived.

It had been nearly a decade since I had last seen Mama, and I anticipated her arrival with excitement.

When I saw her, I was struck by two things: how much she had aged — the gray obvious around her hairline, the lines on her face telling of the hardships she had survived — and how undimmed was her beauty, despite her age. Her green eyes still shone brightly from her olive face; her shape was slim but curved just so at breast and hip. The journey with her two children had been hard on her, but she greeted me with a tired smile, released her older boy's hand,

and enveloped me in a hug I had long wished for, her younger child caught up in the embrace between us. I melted in her arms as the tears streamed down both our faces. The separation of mother and child for so many years was finally overcome.

As for my brothers, I was surprised at the similarities we shared — and how alike they were to Rose as well. I had never met my mother's husband, and I strained to find him in As'ad and Adiib's faces. They looked so much like my own family, with green eyes and shy smiles.

I had been concerned about how Rose would respond to her extended family. Though we associated with many of Wadii's colleagues and had friends of our own, we had mostly been a self-sufficient family of three, relying only on the servants to provide any additional care for our baby. And our friends and acquaintances, mostly English, did not have children Rose's age. I had no idea how she would interact with her young uncles.

But I need not have worried. As'ad was gentle and kind with Rose; I suppose he had learned how to behave around his younger brother. And Adiib and Rose, separated in age by only seven weeks, took to one another with joy and fervor. Indeed, they were similar enough that they might have been mistaken for twins. The three of them together would entertain each other while Mama and I talked over the decade we had spent apart and worked excitedly to prepare for the baby who was on his way. In this way, weeks sped by as I basked in my mother's attentions and love.

One morning, after Wadii' had gone to work, Mama and I were in the kitchen feeding the children their breakfasts. As'ad and Rose were enjoying sandwiches of pita bread and *lebneh*, Rose gumming the bread and sucking out the tart *labneh*. But Adiib refused to eat. Not usually a petulant child, we worried over him as he whined and cried about every morsel he was offered.

"Perhaps he is not well, Mama," I finally ventured. She picked him up and nuzzled him close to her chest, burying her face into the nape of his neck to feel his temperature with her lips.

"*Ye ye ye, habiibi*," she exclaimed. "He is very, very warm."

"What's wrong with him?" I asked.

"I don't know," she replied. "I'll take him to bed with a cool cloth, and we'll see how he feels in a few hours."

By the afternoon, the malady made itself known. First a few red spots appeared on his chest and stomach, then more on his hands and legs. And then more and more quickly the measles spread until he was covered with them.

Of course, we kept Rose well away from the room in which Adiib shivered and sweated through the disease. As'ad had already had the measles and had recovered well a year ago. But Adiib and Rose were both young still. I prayed for Adiib's recovery even as I did everything possible to keep Rose from getting ill.

But it wasn't enough. Less than a week after Adiib's symptoms erupted, Rose had a high fever, and the telltale spots followed quickly on its heels.

Adiib's illness never became too worrisome, and I trusted that Rose would weather it equally well. Still, I worried. The losses of her three older siblings stayed with me, and my faith faltered whenever the shadow of death appeared.

My anxiety grew when it became clear that Rose was unable to fight off the illness as easily as her uncle-cousin. Her health worsened; her fever refused to break, and she developed a hacking cough, never able to catch a full breath. Finally, Wadii', petrified for his beloved daughter, insisted on taking her to the hospital. So we left my mother at home with her boys and went to the missionaries' hospital in the city's center.

When we arrived, the nurses took one look at Rose's pale face and heard her quick, short breaths and immediately admitted her. The measles had caused a severe case of pneumonia, dangerous in one so young. I stayed with her in the hospital for five days as the doctors treated her, and she slowly began to recover. And before she was fully healthy and able to be discharged home, my water broke, and I was taken to deliver my second living child.

BAHI · THE SHINING ONE

Qantarra, 1928

In those days, boys were still preferred, much preferred to girls. Except by my father. Baba always said he wanted girls. After the third daughter, my mother would cry when he said that. All she wanted was a boy, and all she bore were girls.

But I was only the second — of the ones who lived. Mama wasn't quite so desperate for a son yet. Still, she wasn't exactly thrilled when I was born and the nurse announced that it was another girl, so she left the naming of me to my father.

I was born on February 2, 1928, in Qantarra, where my father worked for the railroad company, in the British hospital there, where my mother had been keeping watch at the bedside of my older sister Rose, who was recovering from pneumonia. My father named me Bahi.

Years earlier, when my father was a young man, in his late teens, before his family moved to Haifa, he lived in the village of Shafa 'Amr. And a new minister for the Methodist church came to the town. The minister had come from Lebanon, and the people of Lebanon got education before the Palestinians did because the missionaries came to them first. So the Lebanese minister, a widower, was well educated. As were his daughters.

He brought with him his four beautiful daughters, all well educated and liberated — by the standards of that time and that place. All fair-headed and upper-middle class.

Almost as soon as they arrived, the proposals of marriage began. The young men of the village streamed to the door of the manse, asking for the hands of the daughters of the Methodist minister. And all being of marriageable age, they quickly found husbands among their many suitors. All except the youngest. She was the most beautiful and the most proud. And her name was Bahia.

Of course, my father loved her immediately. It was not in his nature to allow his feelings the time and space to grow. He had always — and would always, until the end of his life — put his faith in love. He trusted that love was never an emotion to be entered into hesitantly, even if it was risky. He loved fully, passionately, all the time. It would be like that when he met my mother years later, when he welcomed his children — even and especially his daughters — in all the years after that. Ever the optimist, he dove into love unflinchingly. And it was so the first time, too, with Bahia.

As I say, she was the most beautiful among her sisters. Her long light brown hair held a tint of auburn in it and framed a face pale enough to look English. In the summer sun, it turned faintly pink. But her eyes were a dark black beneath thick, well-trimmed brows the same color as her hair. And above the pert peak of her lips was a small button nose, easily turned up with her own sense of superiority.

Yes, Bahia was beautiful — and she knew it. She knew, too, that she was desired, and she reveled haughtily in it. She gathered the love of her admirers about her like a bouquet of flowers, which she momentarily regarded and then tossed aside to brown and wither and die.

But my father's love was persistent. He would loiter on the dusty road a few meters from the manse, waiting for a glimpse of Bahia as she went about her errands, a basket nestled into the crook of her elbow. He knew she was well educated, but so was he. The eldest son of a schoolmaster, Wadii' had been sent to Jerusalem on scholarship to one of the missionaries' schools. Even as a very young man, he was well read and well spoken in both English and Arabic.

He would spy her walking home, the basket swinging, her fair head left bare, and come alongside her, offering to carry the basket for her (she never let him), asking about her day in impeccable English (she'd never answer), murmuring his admiration to her (which she always ignored). And then, one day, he elicited a smile from her pink lips, and he felt all his efforts had been rewarded.

The next morning, he sent his father to the manse to ask for her hand in marriage. By the afternoon, the minister's family had returned her answer: Wadii' had been utterly rejected. Bahia refused to marry him.

A few months later, Wadii's family moved to Haifa for the better opportunities, the better life the city had to offer. And the minister's family moved back to Lebanon not long after that. They never heard what happened to Bahia, whether she ever found a suitor she considered worthy.

But Bahia's beauty lingered in Wadii's mind, like the memory of a fragrance.

When I was born, my mother, desiring a son and discovering a daughter, left the naming of me to my father. He looked at me in the freshness of my infancy and loved me. And he said, "How her beauty shines! We will name her Bahi."

THE SNAKE
A STORY

In those days, even if you were wealthy and had servants and housemaids to help you, no one stayed away from their family for too long. The husband might go somewhere else to work and earn money to feed his wife and his children, but he would always come back. And it was better if he could work in the same place as his family. In those days, you stayed close to your clan. The women would have the help of their mothers and sisters to look after the children, and the men relied on their ties of kinship to provide support.

And so, after Bahi's birth, Wadii' and Aniiseh both were ready to return to Haifa, to Wadii's family there. Because he worked for the railroad company, Wadii' was able to ask for a transfer, and they gave it to him. So they took their two girls and moved back home.

At first, they lived with Wadii's parents in their house. Aniiseh hated it. She loved her in-laws — unlike her own family, they had always welcomed her despite her parentage. But Wardeh, her mother-in-law, had only recently reached the age when babies stopped arriving. Like Aniiseh, Wadii' had siblings the same age as his own children, and the house, though spacious, was crowded. But mostly, Aniiseh disliked not being the mistress of her home. She had grown used to the luxuries of having her own space, her own servants, her own dominion — at least where the household was concerned.

So Wadii' quickly set about acquiring land to build a new home for his family. At the time, Mount Carmel was a forested wilderness on the outskirts of Haifa. But a land agent convinced Wadii' that it would be a good investment to buy land there.

At first, Wadii' hesitated. "No one lives there. It is inhabited only by snakes and jackals."

"Now, perhaps," the agent replied. "But wait and see. In just a few years' time, Mount Carmel will be a highly sought-after place to live. You'll get the land for cheap, and you'll have to clear it, but you will not regret the purchase."

Often afterward — but before the *nakba* — Wadii' would think of the agent and recite the quick prayer for him: *may your eyes be blessed*. For the agent's vision of the future was clear. Even today, in what is now called Israel, the homes on Mount Carmel are among the most expensive. Were he alive, were his children and children's children allowed to return to the family home that still belongs to them, they would be wealthy indeed.

But then, when he first bought the land, it was nothing but trees and big boulders and rocky, dusty ground. They used dynamite to clear it. The workers would set the sticks of dynamite in the area they wanted to clear and lay out the long wire for many meters. And then one of them would yell as loudly as he could, "*Baaroood! Baaroood!*" "Explosives! Explosives!" to ensure that no one was nearby, and they would light the fuse and the loud explosion would take place, and the rocks would be smashed and the trees toppled, and the workers would cart it all away before moving to a new area and starting it all over again.

In this way, they cleared the land for the first few homes on Mount Carmel, including Wadii's, nearer the bottom, and others going upward on large terraces.

At first, Wadii' built a small house with two bedrooms, a bathroom, a kitchen, and a small living room. It was only a start. They would add on more and more in time and as his family grew. But it was enough for him and Aniiseh and their two girls, Rose and Bahi. At least Aniiseh would be happy to move from her husband's family's home and into her own place, he thought.

But Aniiseh was not happy; it had been years since they were wed, but Wadii' still had to work harder than ever before to elicit the shy smile from his wife. And the home he built for her on Mount Carmel didn't do it. They would wake together in the mornings, and as he readied himself for work, he would see her in the kitchen, lightly hitting her own cheeks with the palms of her hands in a sign of desperation, mumbling about living among the wild animals, the snakes and jackals outside their door. By the time they moved in, she was well into her next pregnancy, and she disdained to bring her child — *it* must *be a son this time*, she thought — into this wilderness instead of the well-appointed home he deserved.

And then one day, Wadii' came home to find his daughters undressed and whining in the small sala, their mother, who usually cared so well for the girls, distraught on the settee, moaning into her hands, her swollen belly protruding through her arms. His heart leapt into his throat; he barely dared to ask her what was wrong. Finally, he plucked up the courage to cross to his Aniiseh and take her in his arms: "*Yamma. In shallah kheyr. Shuu malik ya habiibti, ya Aniiseh?* What's wrong?"

At first, he couldn't make sense of much — something about a snake and a daughter. He peered at Rose and Bahi still whimpering near his feet; they weren't entirely happy, but they didn't seem to be suffering from snakebite either.

And then the whole story tumbled through Aniiseh's tears, and Wadii' had to stifle his laughter. Aniiseh had been outside with the girls, hanging the clothes on the line. All of a sudden, movement on the ground ahead of her caught her attention. When she looked closer, she saw the snake, a harmless one, slithering along the topsoil. It was headed in her direction, and she could see its beady eyes clearly. It looked straight at her, stopped, and quickly changed direction to speed wiggling away.

It was an old wives' tale, familiar and proven enough that even Wadii' knew it. If a snake sees a pregnant woman and raises its head, the child in the mother's womb is a boy. If the snake runs away, a girl is born.

Wadii' held his wife against his chest and comforted her. Surreptitiously, he slid his hand around to the side of her belly and stroked his unborn child. He didn't believe in such nonsense; he would love whatever new life grew in Aniiseh's womb — he loved the child already. But as he held her to him and looked at his beautiful daughters who had calmed in their father's presence, he found himself hoping the snake was right and he would soon welcome another girl, with her mother's eyes and Wadii's own sense of humor, into his family.

Abla was born only a few weeks later. By then, Aniiseh had resigned herself to the idea of another daughter and loved her. But Wadii' was as smitten and passionate as ever. When they laid her in his arms, he held the baby close to his heart and smiled into eyes as dark and beautiful as his own. "*Bintii*," he whispered. "My daughter."

THE BOY
A STORY

In those days, the people knew the Holy Scriptures. From a young age, we were taught by the missionaries to memorize whole verses, whole sections by heart and to recite them. And we knew the stories of the Bible, too, so that the events in the lives of our ancestors of faith shaped us as surely as our own family's experiences.

When Aniiseh, now mother to five girls, Rose, Bahi, Abla, Nuha, and Leila, fell pregnant again and began her refrain of longing for a son, she expected her husband to reprimand her. How was it possible that he — a man! — could be so happy with daughters, only ever daughters, she wondered. How infuriating that, with each pregnancy, he refused to join her in her fervent prayers for a boy.

But something was different this time. When she told Wadii' that her bleeding had not come, that she prayed, this time, God would grant them a son, Wadii' smiled at her and responded, simply, "*In shallah*," God willing. And for once, she smiled back at him.

And then, just a few weeks later, as they undressed in the evening for bed, Wadii' began speaking to her: "Do you remember the story of Hannah?" he said. And he reminded her, weaving the story between them like a symbol of hope, like a dream, finally, shared.

Hannah was the much-beloved first wife of Elkanah, the Levite. Though he loved her more than his second wife Peninnah, Elkanah could not show his love through the gifts and sacrifices like those he gave on behalf of Peninnah, for unlike her sister-wife, Hannah was barren. She had been married to Elkanah for over a decade, but Hannah's womb still refused to bear its fruit. And while Hannah was comforted by her husband's love for her, she was plagued daily, hourly, by Peninnah's combined jealousy and superiority, the constant, pointed reminders she made of the many children she had given to their shared husband.

And so Hannah prayed fervently to the Lord, that he might take pity on her, to put an end to her barrenness and her grief and to grant her the child she longed for. And the Lord heard her prayer. She conceived a child and delivered him. And they named him Samuel. And when the child was weaned, Hannah took him to the temple, to the care of the priest Eli, to be dedicated to the service of God in thanksgiving that the Lord had heard her prayer and remembered her.

As he finished the story, Wadii' turned to Aniiseh, lying on her bed, her hands resting lightly on the slight roundness of her belly. "Pray, *habiibti*," he told her. "Pray to God. What he wills will be done. And this time, I know, we will be given a son. He will be called Samuel."

He arrived late. Aniiseh carried him through forty weeks and then nearly two weeks more. When he finally arrived, the whole neighborhood rejoiced. None knew joy like Aniiseh's, of course. She cradled her son against her chest, felt his gummy clamp on her breast and let her salty, joyful tears flow as freely as her milk. God had remembered her.

And when the forty days were complete, they welcomed the friends and neighbors who shared in their joy, the celebrations of all their kith and kin. For weeks, the well-wishers streamed through the main sala of the house on Mount Carmel and left again, carrying small bags of Jordan almonds as a gift of thanksgiving for their sympathetic salutations. And Samuel's older sisters went to school followed by the household servants, carrying baskets with bags of almonds to share with their friends and peers. The Habiibi family must have spent a fortune in candy-coated pastel almonds, but no expense was spared. The eldest son of the Habiibis finally had a son of his own.

Perhaps, in some families, such enthusiasm over the birth of a boy might have caused jealousy among the older girls. But the daughters of Wadii' had always been beloved by their parents, even as they knew their mother's longing for a son. They welcomed and doted on Samuel from the moment of his birth. He grew up strong and certain of his family's love — from the sisters that came before *and* after him — and from the parents that prayed to God for his existence. And he took seriously the responsibility, the calling on his life that he knew such love demanded. Like his namesake, Samuel would dedicate his life to the Lord who had knit him together from his parents' prayers in his mother's womb. Even as a child, he knew he would be a priest in God's church.

When he was still young, Sami — as he was nicknamed — attended a school in Haifa run by Anglican missionaries. But his family fled the violence and turmoil of the *nakba* in 1948 when he was just twelve years old. They spent a short time in Egypt and then settled in Damascus, where Sami finished his preliminary schooling. Then, obedient to God's call on his life, he sought a path to ordination in the Anglican Church.

But Sami's father, having fled the violence of Palestine and started over in Damascus with a young family, had no money to provide additional schooling to his only son. And Sami was left with few choices to pursue his vocation. He found a way forward through the Lutheran Church. If he taught in one of their missionary schools in Bethlehem for a year, the church would grant him a scholarship to pursue a divinity degree, from start to finish, in their seminary in Germany. Once his studies were complete, Sami could be ordained a priest in his own Anglican tradition. He jumped at the chance.

Sami moved away from his family and returned to his homeland, to Bethlehem, in Palestine, to teach in the school there. After his year of service, having received the promised scholarship, he set out for Germany. All of nineteen years old, on the heels of a turbulent and transient youth, Sami bravely boarded a plane for the first time in his life that would take him to the next chapter of his vocation; he enrolled that fall at Augustana Divinity School in the town of Neuendettelsau — a place he could hardly pronounce.

But pronunciation, despite some background in German, proved to be the least of Sami's problems after his arrival. Though the faculty and students of Augustana were welcoming, the culture shock of his surroundings quickly became a significant hurdle. The language, the climate, the methods of study were all new to the Palestinian youth, desperate to fulfill his calling but so far from home. He ached for the familiar sounds of Arabic. Linguistically isolated, he had no friends among his peers.

Plus, as he labored to complete the seminary's assignments, he labored, too, under misguided notions of piety and priesthood. He thought that in order to become a priest and preach to others, he had to be sin-free himself. No one at the school contradicted his misconception of Scripture or challenged his notion of what it takes to be a minister to God's people. He felt lost, adrift from his own identity, missing so much of who he was. And then the winter set in.

Accustomed as Sami was to the bright sun and warm weather of the Middle East, the dark, frigid days and nights of that German January battered him with a loneliness like he had never before known. It was too much for him. Crippled beneath the pressure of his own high expectations and the darkness that threatened him within and without, Samuel left the school of theology, left Germany, left his hope of ordination. He returned home to his family in Damascus before Easter.

It felt to him like the worst kind of failure. The sense of responsibility, of his broken vocation, weighed heavily on his heart. He felt as though he was not only disappointing himself but also disobeying his parents and denying his God. He would never become an ordained priest; he would never fulfill the promise his parents made to the Lord; he would never be the man he was meant to be. Quitting seminary felt like the worst sin imaginable.

But he was still a young man and took on the responsibilities of his adulthood. He worked for a time in Damascus and then acquired a loan and enrolled in the American University of Beirut, three years behind other youth his age.

Eventually, he met and married a pretty Lebanese girl and raised two children, a girl and a boy. He was deeply invested in the Anglican church of which he was a member, worshiping in the pews every Sunday, volunteering his time and talents, tithing his money for the mission of God. And wherever his career took him, he worked diligently, honestly, and with integrity. But he never lost sight of that which he saw as his failure. He prayed that God might forgive the promise he had broken, the faltering steps that kept him from an ordained vocation and a life lived in service to God's church.

In time, the opportunity arose for him to immigrate to the United States, and he took advantage of it. Once again, he left the Middle East, this time permanently, and ventured into a new life, trusting in the God he clung to.

And he wasn't the only one of his family to do so. Indeed, In'aam, one of his eight sisters, had already emigrated and had settled with her husband in the outskirts of Houston, Texas — a place whose climate, at least, was reminiscent of that of their childhood. And slowly, many others of the Habiibi clan came, too. Sami brought with him his mother Aniiseh, who lived with them for a while, and afterward came Rose and Bahi, Abla and Nuha, and eventually, his youngest sister Elham. Some of his sisters brought family with them; others followed their own grown children to the States and settled in the Texas suburb. And Sami watched in wonder as his extended family grew around him: his own children and his sisters' kids, who in turn grew up and married and had children of their own.

Most of Sami's sisters had married men of other Christian faiths and had taken on those traditions. So Sunday mornings saw the Habiibi clan worshiping the same God at different churches in the neighborhood: Catholic and Baptist and Episcopalian. His oldest siblings, Rose and Bahi, though, had both married Anglican men when they were still young women in Haifa, so they and their families attended Saint Dunstan's Episcopal Church in Houston alongside Sami. Bahi and her husband Fariid sat in the first pew on the wide right-hand side of the sanctuary. Next to them was Rose with her grown son, Kamil, who had long been nonverbal due to Down syndrome. Behind them was May, Bahi's daughter and Sami's niece, who brought her two little girls, Zeyna and Leyla, with her each Sunday. And behind them, in the third pew, sat Sami, his wife Lena always by his side, his two by now teenagers only sometimes also there.

How Sami enjoyed worship. He always felt enlivened by it. Though the service was in English, though the people behind and to the left of him were much whiter than those who worshiped beside him in his youth, the liturgy was as familiar as ever. He could often sing the hymns in his native tongue. The rhythm of God's love for him echoed in the repetition of movements he had always known: to bow to the cross of the crucified one, to sit and receive the word of the Lord, to kneel for the confession, to stand to profess one's faith and sing the praises of God, to watch as the priest lifted the host, broke it, and held it out to him, to all of them, a sign of that great love that had carried Sami through so much loss to so many blessings.

And then to walk forward to the altar rail and to kneel before the broken body of his Lord, to hold out his hands in supplication and expectation, to hear the sacred words, "the body and blood of Christ which was given for thee; preserve thy body and soul unto everlasting life; take and eat this in remembrance that Christ died for thee and be thankful"; and to taste and see that the Lord was oh so good, even in the face of Sami's own failures. He would go back to his pew, kneel down, and let his gaze travel over the bowed heads of his sisters and their families before him, and he was thankful indeed.

And nourished in soul by the eucharistic feast, Sami would look forward to the bodily nourishment that his sisters always provided. Every Sunday, without fail, the Habiibi siblings would gather from their various churches at one of the sisters' homes. They all brought with them their families — their husbands and children and grandchildren. The day's hostess would have worked half the week preparing the food: hard-boiled eggs, squeaky white cheeses, warm *manaiish*, soft Arabic dips and spreads — hummus and *fuul* and *baba ghanoush* — and of course, American coffee and dozens of the round, flat loaves of Arabic bread.

As the patriarch, Sami sat at the head of the dining room table. Children ran around him, asking for their mothers' help to pile their plates with food; his brothers-in-law yelled at the ref of the soccer match playing in Spanish in the living room; his sisters and their daughters chattered about school and work, cooking and child-rearing. And he would look at them all, at the joyful chaos around him, and utter a quiet thanksgiving for the goodness of the Lord.

He picked up a loaf of the pita in one of the many bread baskets that adorned any of his sisters' tables for the meal. He gazed at its perfect roundness, the shades of white and brown that reminded him of the childhood streets of his Haifa home. Slowly, joyfully, he folded the bread down the middle, the edges tearing apart first to reveal the white warmth within as Sami's brown hands worked their way down. He took the bread and broke it.

He smiled, kept one half on his plate and passed the other to whoever sat beside him — his sister or his wife, a nephew or niece, or one of their many, many children.

And then he would start asking questions of those around him: What did you do this week? Where did you go? Who did you meet? What do you think of the new film that just came out? Have you read this book? What are you studying in school these days?

No matter who was near him on any given day, his courteous curiosity would engage them all — young or old, male or female, blood relative or one of his many white in-laws, it didn't matter. He was interested and involved in their lives, in their ideas, in their challenges, in their joys. He listened to them attentively and responded thoughtfully. When a youngster needed guidance, he would offer it gently; if a sister needed sympathy, he would give it unstintingly; when a nephew expressed anxiety, he would provide comfort and reassurance. He was by no means perfect, but he was fully present to them all.

And it wasn't just his family. When his friends or acquaintances were lost or sick or suffering, he would take them out to lunch at his favorite local deli and would listen to them and advise them, comfort them and give them hope.

Like a good shepherd, he tended to the ones God had given him as best he could. Decades after he had left the German seminary, he was still grappling faithfully with his sense of calling.

When the cancer was diagnosed, he was only in his sixties. It was a palpable shock at first, as these things always are. There seemed to still be so much life left in him, so much life left to live. How could he leave his wife and children, his sisters and their families, so soon? But Sami had always been a man of faith, always tried, as best he could, to be obedient to God's will for him. And death, he realized, must not be any different. If God was calling him home, he would not go stubbornly but willingly, graciously, faithfully.

Near the end, he lay on what would become his deathbed in his house in the foreign country that had finally welcomed him and claimed him as one of its own. One of his nieces came to see him that day, his great-niece, in fact. Leyla, May's daughter, the granddaughter of his sister Bahi. It had been Bahi who, a year earlier, had shared the good news with Sami that surprised and delighted him: "Leyla is going to be a minister," she had told him. "She has started the process to be ordained as an Episcopal priest."

Now his light-skinned great-niece sits by his bed, telling him of her plans for seminary in New England, asking for his blessing, in not so many words. And he closes his eyes and smiles with satisfaction, a benediction in its own right. God's wonders are many, and his blessings are manifold. Sami prays that Leyla will see the process through with ease. He knows his body will never make it that long, but he wishes he could be present on the day of her ordination. But then again, maybe, in some unknown way, he will be.

There is a lull in the conversation, and Leyla and her great-uncle Sami sit in silence with one another for a moment. When she speaks again, her voice is almost a whisper. "Are you scared, *Khalo*?" she asks him. And he lets her question hang, briefly, unanswered as he turns his gaze inward, scanning his heart and mind to see whether there is fear, but he discovers, somewhat surprisingly, that only courage and contentment dwell there. He finds that his trust in God's mercy and forgiveness, his faith in God's love for him has come through at the last.

Finally he looks at her, catching her green eyes, so like Bahi's, filled now with concern and worry and grief. And he smiles his reassurance. "No, *habiibti*," he tells her. "I am sad to be leaving my family; I am sorry that I will not be here as I have always enjoyed being, but I am not scared. I am going home to be with my Lord and Savior. I am going home to be with my fellow Galilean."

And she reaches across the space before her to his brown hand lying on the bed and squeezes her "amen."

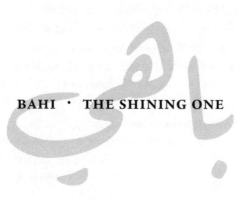

BAHI · THE SHINING ONE

Haifa, 1938

In those days, there was no coeducation. Boys went to school with other boys, and girls went to school with other girls. Even when I was small, we were taught separately from one another.

At first, before my brother was born, my parents sent me to the church school that was part of the Anglican mission. When I was a little girl of six or seven, a new church was being built. They gave the basement of the church for the school, and they built the church itself above. And that was the school I was sent to.

But my mother would warn us, my sister Rose and I, in the early days of our schooling: "Don't you dare misbehave," she said. "If you misbehave, if you are naughty, if you make your instructors unhappy with you, you will bring dishonor on our family. And it will kill me. If you give them trouble, I will die of the shame, and you will be orphans without a mother." Looking back now, I see how real of a threat it must have seemed to her; perhaps her whole life she imagined that her own misbehavior as a child led, somehow, to her mother's expulsion all those years ago. And it seemed a real threat to me, her young daughter, too. I took her at her word.

It was soon after the start of the school year that work on the church above the basement-school was completed, and they started holding services there. Weddings and funerals and baptisms. And in those days, anytime there was a funeral, they would toll the bell of the church, slowly, deliberately. *Dong. Dong. Dong. Dong.* And anytime the funeral bell rang, my heart skipped a beat and I would wrack my brain, rehearse my behavior during the day, consider in stark terms whether I had been truly obedient to my teachers and attentive to my tasks. Or had I been naughty, and had my misbehavior been reported back to my mother already? Was it her death that the church's bell was tolling?

And I would cry to myself, silently, hiding my tears in my arms, for I feared that the teacher would scold me.

But I was not long in the church school with its tolling bell and the anxiety I felt.

My brother was born in December of 1937 and my father thought that there were too many children for my mother to care for. So it was decided that, the following fall, Rose and I would be sent to the boarding school in Ramallah. I was ten years old.

Early in the year, we began our preparations. My parents bought the required uniforms for our new school. Rose and I each received two sets. A blue tunic overlay and underneath a white top: a short-sleeved blouse for the summers and a warm, long-sleeved jersey for the winters, for Ramallah was very, very cold in the winter, and it always snows.

We had mixed feelings about going away to school, my sister and I. The concept of boarding school was entirely new and foreign to us. And neither Rose nor I took change well. Our matriculation into the Ramallah Friends School would be the first time we would ever sleep away from our family's home. And it wouldn't be for just a night or two. Only during the infrequent holidays would we come back to Haifa.

But despite all the uncertainty we faced, we were excited, too. As the oldest siblings, we were being given an opportunity that our younger sisters were unlikely to receive. And while Rose and I didn't always get along — I think she had been spoiled by my father since the day she was born — we loved each other and had learned to rely upon each other as we had grown. We felt glad to be taking on this new adventure together. We saw it as a coming-of-age of sorts.

But near the end of the summer, as we counted down the last few weeks until our departure, I got sick. I came down with the typhoid fever. There was no medicine for typhoid then, and some children suffered bodily damage or brain damage, or, like my mother's brother, even death. But thank God, not me. I was sick, though, and had to recuperate naturally. My mother kept my younger siblings away from me and fed me fluids constantly to rid me of the illness. School opened mid-September, but I was still not fully well and had to stay in bed one more week.

Of course, my parents could not incur the expense of taking two trips to Ramallah, so my illness delayed Rose's matriculation, too. She was so angry with me! She started scolding me and hitting me and saying bad words to me because we had to postpone our trip.

In that period, the Arabs began to have a sense of the way in which the British winds were blowing. We had welcomed them, with their wealth and their wisdom, after the dinginess of the Ottoman Empire, but already, by the middle of the 1930s, there was talk of a coming upheaval, a hint of the sacrifice that would be demanded of us, extracted from us, for the sake of the European Jews who came at the invitation of the British.

By the time I left for boarding school, there were Arab revolters who operated among us — not the revolutionaries who would fight on our behalf, but revolters. Angry and misguided militants who forced Arab men to wear the Palestinian headdress and who forced the women to wear the hijab, even the Christian women.

So in preparation for our journey to Ramallah, my mother bought us all scarves to wrap around our heads and cover our hair — one each for her and for Rose and for me. My mother's mother came with her son to stay with my other sisters. And my parents, my baby brother Sami and Rose and I, with our headdresses and scarves and our luggage with our new clothes and shoes, towels and linens and sheets, boarded a bus in Haifa. We took the bus from Haifa to Jerusalem. And then from Jerusalem to Ramallah we took a taxi.

When we arrived at the school, one of the teachers met us and took us into the dormitories, which were upstairs, above the classrooms. There were two halls of dormitories, one for the elementary students and one for the older girls, in secondary school.

We were each assigned a bed. Rose was number thirty-seven, and I was number thirty-eight, for all of our years at the school. Our numbers were everywhere: posted on our beds in the dormitory and sewn into every item of clothing that we had. We put up our clothes in small cupboards (also numbered, of course) beside each bed as our parents watched.

And then, the time came to say goodbye. We had been excited, my sister and I, to start the term in our new school. But when our parents left us to return home, our excitement disappeared. As soon as our family left the room, Rose started crying at the top of her voice: "No! Mama! Baba! I want to go back!"

As for me, I was filled with apprehension. This massive change scared me. But most of all, I missed my baby brother. He was not yet a year old when I went to boarding school, and I had helped my mother greatly in the raising of him thus far. He was special to me, and I hated to be separated from him.

But unlike Rose, I didn't cry or complain. I've never been one to show my feelings. Perhaps because of my mother's early threats, I was always afraid that too much emotion expressed would have dire consequences.

But what a difference boarding school was from what we had known. At our home, there was always chaos. It was joyful and love-filled, but it was chaotic: my siblings and the servants and my mother's pessimism and my father's constant optimism. We were always pulled in different directions, by other people's needs and other people's emotions.

Boarding school, by contrast, was all discipline and order. And that school taught me to love discipline.

The school was run by the American Friends, the Quakers. They taught us geography, mathematics, reading, and writing, but they also taught us etiquette and good manners and how to keep a bank book and how to hold conversation with all sorts of people. And the Christian Scriptures, too, of course, even though there were a number of Muslim girls in the school, from the wealthiest Palestinian families.

Rose and I were both together in the fifth grade. Rose was never much of a student. Not that she wasn't smart, but she hated to study. And I loved it. I was always the top of my class. So early on, my teachers had moved me up a grade.

Rose's lack of studiousness eventually caught up with her. We attended school together for the first three years. As usual, I studied hard and worked to please my teachers. But Rose found friends among the girls who were not so serious; instead of studying, they would gossip and socialize. Her grades suffered because of it, and nothing my father said to her changed her behavior. Finally, one summer, when Rose and I were home for the holidays, he gathered all of us sisters together and looked into our faces, one by one.

"You are well-educated girls," he told us. "Not all girls receive the opportunities that we provide for you. You must understand that. So I expect you to study hard and do well in your schooling. Any daughter of mine who fails her classes will not be allowed to attend school." His eyes landed on Rose and lingered there for a number of awkward moments. Rose colored and stared down at her shoes. Surely, I thought, she would refocus her energies now and become a better student.

But it was not to be. She failed her first year of high school. My father followed through with his threat; he refused to pay twice for the same education, and Rose left school. Had it been me, I would have been distraught, to leave my beloved school, my beloved teachers. But Rose was happy. The disciplined environment and strict rules had never fit her well, and she was eager for the bit of independence that having a job might bring.

Plus, her education had prepared her well enough to teach younger students, and she got a job as a kindergarten teacher, which she was very good at. She worked alongside a woman who would eventually become her mother-in-law.

Rose left school in the spring of 1940; World War II had already begun. We hadn't been exactly wealthy beforehand, but my father had a good job, and we never wanted for things. But then the war started, and everything became hard to find: food and thread for sewing our clothes and everything, even cash.

So that fall, when I went to school by myself this time, without my sister beside me, I carried no check from my father to pay for the fees. And no note, either, to explain the circumstances.

When I arrived at the school, as was the custom, the principal called me to her office to welcome me back and to receive the money that would pay for my schooling that year. Her name was Ms. Hannush. She was strict and had a bitter disposition. But she liked me, because I was always obedient. Still, I did not relish the thought of explaining my situation to her.

"*Ahlan wa sahlan, ya* Bahi," she greeted me as I entered. "It is good to have you back among us this semester." When our formal pleasantries were complete, she asked me for my father's check. And I was so scared. I spoke in a whisper. "I'm sorry, Ms. Hannush. My father did not send me with a check this time."

I dared not look up, dared not look into her eyes, dared not show my fear.

"So you have no payment for your fees?" I met her question with my silence. "In that case, we will send you back to your home. There is no place for you here," she said.

The blood in my veins turned to antifreeze, both tingling hot and burning cold. It was impossible that I could leave my school; I couldn't think of the journey back, of boarding the bus for the three-hour ride home, of the end to everything that I loved. But how could I refute the principal's statement? We had always been taught not to talk back to our teachers; to disagree, to express our desires or opinions was seen as taboo. And I who, more than any of my family, kept my feelings to myself, how could I say to Ms. Hannush how this departure would impact me, how it would break me?

So I said nothing at all. But I started to cry. And for once, I was unable to hide my emotions. Ms. Hannush cleared her throat, and when I looked up at her, the tears were streaming down my cheeks. And I saw the pity on her face. For a moment, her lips tightened into a straight line and then she breathed a heavy sigh.

"There are no funds left for a scholarship for you," she said. "What little money we had for these things has ceased to exist in these trying times. But you can stay on as a work scholar if you can keep up with your studies. Do you know what a work scholar is?"

I shook my head.

"Poor girls like you," she went on. She really said that. "Poor girls like you who have no money for their education work for their education."

So that was the first year that I worked alongside my studies. My main job was to help the little girls in the school with their lessons and their routines. During the evening study hours, from seven to nine o'clock every night, I would take charge of the little girls: I helped with their homework, and I would take them upstairs to the dormitories and make sure they changed their clothes and their underpants, brushed their teeth and their hair, and washed their faces, and I settled them into bed. An hour later, when I had finally finished these tasks, I would go back downstairs and tend to my own studies in the little time that was left to me.

The work added to my tasks, but I didn't mind it so much. I enjoyed the smaller children, and I had a gift for teaching and helping them. And though the job ate into my own study hours, I was clever enough that I could manage.

But the work marked a change in my position — a change that did not go unnoticed by my peers. I had friends in school, but, because I did not socialize like Rose did, because I was shyer and less expressive, I was not close to the other girls in the same way that Rose had been. Besides, I always believed that too much intimacy breeds contempt. But perhaps not enough intimacy has the same result. The other girls my age knew that only poor students had to work for their schooling, and they looked down upon me for it. And I did not like that.

The Second World War would form the backdrop of the whole of my secondary school career. The fees for my education were not the only thing that was scarce then. Food, clothing, even labor were all hard to come by. Everything was rationed, and anything of any quality or good use was sent to the armed forces fighting in the war.

Even my school, which was American, of course, felt the pinch. The good foods of my early years disappeared. We were fed a thin diet of cheap things. Gone were the daily vegetables and weekly meat meals. They didn't even cook rice for us, for that was a commodity demanded by the soldiers at the front, and they gave us bulgur — the poor man's substitute — instead. I didn't touch meat for all those years. The only fish we ate was saltfish that came to us from the gulf. It was so salty that they would have to soak it in big barrels of water for a whole day, changing out the water three times to rid the fish of some of its saltiness. But it was never enough.

Our Sunday breakfast "treat" was a piece of very brown, almost black bread, with a small amount of margarine — not butter, of course — and a drizzle of homemade honey, which wasn't real honey but a substitute made in the kitchens from dark sugar. And one cup of tea for each girl. That was it. And that was on Sundays only!

Some of the girls who came from wealthier families — or families who had fewer children than mine to feed and clothe, at least — received special treats from their parents who visited them or sent their gifts through the post. There was a cupboard in the school kitchens where these tins and boxes of personal food were allowed to be kept, each box marked with the name and number of the girl it belonged to. I never had such treats; my family was too poor to send them. But sometimes one of the girls would share her snack with me. I would accept gratefully but guiltily, since I knew I would never be able to repay the favor.

And then, one day, in my third year in the high school, my parents came to visit me. It was the only time they made the journey to see me in all my years there, save for my matriculation alongside Rose and my graduation at the end. I don't remember why they made the trip or how they could have afforded it.

They brought me a tin of *ka'ak*, round, date-filled cookies that my mother had made. Of course, the quality was not as fine because of the rationing, so she had substituted margarine for butter, and the *ka'ak* was a darker color because of the poor quality of sugar that was available to her. But I was excited to receive them.

After my parents left, I thought to myself that if I kept my tin of *ka'ak* in the snack cupboard with all the other girls' tins, it would only forestall the inevitable end of their disappearance, and I didn't want to dole them slowly out to the other girls who had shared their food with me in the past.

So instead, I whispered to the handful of my peers who had been generous to me that my parents had brought me some cookies, and I invited them, surreptitiously, to join me on the balcony of the dormitory after lights-out to partake of the feast. And that's what we did.

But one of the teachers must have seen or heard us whispering as she crossed the courtyard to her own rooms that evening, and she reported us to the principal.

Every morning of school started the same way: the whole school gathered in the assembly hall for what we called "prayer assembly." We sang hymns and said a few prayers each morning, and one of the teachers would give a short address. The assembly ended with school-wide announcements. And the morning after my little *ka'ak* party on the balcony, Ms. Hannush ended her announcements at the podium by saying, "Last night, some naughty girls were seen and heard past the hour for bed talking together on the balcony of the dormitory. Please stand up now if you were among these girls."

The assembly went quiet. I felt the red bloom of shame rise from my stomach up through my chest, past my fast-beating heart, through my throat and finally into my cheeks. My eyes stung with unshed tears, and for a brief moment, I wondered whether I had the courage to do what I knew must be done. But before I could doubt myself entirely, I gathered my feet under me and rose, putting my hand up in the air, elbow slightly bent, to show Ms. Hannush that I had something to say. I stood alone, and the principal called my name. "Bahi Habiibi?" she asked, surprised. "You were among these girls? But I know there were others, too."

Before anyone else could respond, I tried to speak up. "I'm sorry, miss," I began. But my voice came out as an inaudible squeak. I swallowed and tried again. "Please excuse me, Ms. Hannush," I managed, more strongly. The principal's dark eyes bore into me even across the distance of the assembly. "I *was* one of the girls on the balcony. And there *were* others with me. But they should not get in trouble. It was I who invited them. They wouldn't have been there if it wasn't for me. They were there only because I gave them the invitation."

An interminable silence followed. Finally, Ms. Hannush, with brow furrowed, sighed. "All right, Bahi. You will not attend your classes today. Come straight to my office immediately after the assembly is dismissed." The music teacher called the girls to attention to begin the final hymn, and as they all got to their feet around me, I took refuge in the brief moment of anonymity, even while I could discern their whispered wonderings about my fate.

The assembly dispersed, and as the girls around me clattered their way to their classrooms, I slowly shuffled to Ms. Hannush's office. I prayed to God as I walked, pleading with him to grant me strength or to miraculously spirit me away from this moment, or even to let me die. I figured that death would be better than what must await me, because I thought God would be more tender with me than Ms. Hannush.

Her door was closed when I got there, and I hoped I had beaten her to the office and could have a few minutes to collect myself. But my knock was quickly answered by her crisp, "Enter!"

I tentatively opened the door, stepped inside, closed it after me, and stood in the middle of the dull gray tiled floor. "Bahi Habiibi!" She had not raised her voice, but the intensity of disappointment and scolding in her tone was palpable when she said my name. I flinched as though she had hit me. I was better prepared when she repeated it.

"Bahi Habiibi! Of all the girls in the school, you are always the most serious, the most obedient. It is not acceptable that you would do such a thing. What were you doing out there on the balcony with those other girls?"

I explained the situation to her as best I could. I was mortified that I had displeased the principal and petrified that she would send me home for such an infraction, despite my pristine behavior in the past. But when I had finished, she only sighed. "Whatever the intention behind your behavior, you know better than to disobey the rules of this school," she said. "You will not attend classes this morning. Instead, you will stay here and tidy up my office as I make my rounds. I want books straightened and arranged, cabinets dusted, and papers tidied. The floor will be swept and mopped, and the drawers of my desk will be emptied, cleaned, and restored of their contents. Do you understand me?"

My answer came out with a sigh of relief: "Yes, Ms. Hannush."

She gathered a few papers into her arms and crossed the room to the door. Before she left, she turned and pointed to a large freestanding cupboard in the back corner of her office. "Don't concern yourself with what's inside that cabinet," she said. "But I want everything else to be spotless by the time I return before lunch."

I worked tirelessly and happily that morning. I was sorry to miss my classes, but the consequences of my misbehavior were by far lighter than I had expected, and I took the opportunity to read a few paragraphs of some of the more interesting titles on Ms. Hannush's bookshelves. When the principal returned, I was satisfied that I had completed my tasks fully and well. She was satisfied, too, for she glanced around briefly and then nodded. "Go and have your lunch with the other girls," she told me. "But come back here afterward. You won't attend your afternoon classes either."

When I sat down at the table in the dining hall, the other girls crowded around me like ants, desperate to carry away a morsel of gossip. *What was my punishment?* I quietly explained that I had been required to clean Ms. Hannush's office, and the girls, disappointed, quickly left me alone. The meal finished, I returned to the principal.

"The afternoon will give you enough time to clean out that cabinet," she said after I knocked and entered. "It's been full of that stuff for years." She hadn't even lifted her head from her paper and pen as she addressed me. Curious, I walked around her desk to the corner cupboard and opened its two doors. The thing was full of small bags and gold-painted boxes and tiny tins of Jordan almonds, the same candy-coated nuts I had brought to the church school with me when my baby brother was born, the traditional gift of celebration. Shelf after shelf of the cabinet held packets of the sweet treats, jumbled up on top of one another in their various receptacles. I stared at them all in a moment of confounded wonder.

Ms. Hannush must have sensed my confusion. "I get invited to a lot of weddings," she said. "Most of the graduates of the school send me invitations. I go to the weddings and bring back the favors. But I can't stand almonds."

"What shall I do with them all?" I asked. "Throw them away?" It seemed an unconscionable waste to do so. Especially now, when such fine sugar as coated the almonds was so hard to come by — when nuts of any kind, for that matter, were impossible to find.

"No. I don't suppose that would be right," Ms. Hannush replied. "Just empty the cabinet and clean it well and then arrange them back in as best you can for now." She paused and looked up from her desk. "Why don't you take some — as many as you like — for yourself?"

It was a tempting offer, but having such enviable treats as Jordan almonds — when I had just landed myself in such trouble over a tin of simple *ka'ak* — seemed like a risky decision. "No thank you, Ms. Hannush, not for me," I said. "But when the term ends, please may I come back and get some for my siblings? I have four little sisters and a little brother at home, in addition to Rose, of course." My mother had had yet another baby, after Sami — another girl, called Samira — during my tenure at boarding school. "My sisters and brother would be very pleased if I brought them some almonds when I return."

"Yes, yes, of course," she said, her thin lips turning up ever so slightly at the sides. "Take as many as you like."

And I did. When the term ended, with Ms. Hannush's permission, I carefully counted out six packets of Jordan almonds in the six prettiest packages I could find. The rest I left in the corner cupboard. I always wondered what she did with them.

BAHI · THE SHINING ONE

Ramallah, 1943

In those days, teachers were not allowed to be married. If you worked as a teacher in a school, and you got engaged to be married, you were not allowed to continue in your position. All of our teachers were unmarried — even the church school ones. When they got married, they left.

But the boarding-school teachers never got married. Ms. Hannush was the principal of my school the whole time I was a student there. The previous principal, Ms. Jones, Ms. Alice Jones, had retired before my arrival in 1938, but after a brief return to the States, she had come back to volunteer in the school. She taught us Scripture and etiquette, and she was so sweet, the kindest teacher there. I admired her. I wanted to be just like her when I grew up.

And so I was pleased when I was offered the opportunity to take an additional teacher training certificate course in my last two years of high school. I could become a teacher like Ms. Jones, I thought. I happily accepted.

I walked with another of my favorite teachers, Ms. Garnet Guile, to the teacher training college nearby.

This teacher, Ms. Guile, taught only the oldest girls in our school, and I loved her because she treated us like college students, like we were important and intellectual and like our thoughts and opinions mattered. She looked and dressed like a man; she was not pretty. But she was kind, and she introduced us to liberal ideas — or ideas that were liberal for that time, at least — like choosing our own husband or reading literature that was considered too risqué for girls our age. I remember reading Somerset Maugham's *The Razor's Edge* at her suggestion and thinking my father would not approve, but devouring the novel anyway.

And it was this Ms. Guile who used to walk with me to the teacher training college three afternoons per week. While the rest of the girls stayed at the boarding school to attend to the other women's trades available — either sewing and needlework and the like in preparation for household duties or studying for the matriculation test that would allow them to work in governmental offices — I sat in special courses designed to teach us how to teach others. As usual, I drank in the knowledge.

By the start of my last year of school, I was already grieving the thought of leaving. And the teachers didn't want me to leave, either. I am not bragging about this. I know because they asked me to come back to teach at that same school after I graduated.

Ms. Hannush wrote a letter to my father asking his permission for me to become a teacher there. I took it home with me during my final Easter holiday and presented it to my father. I stood before him with bated breath and watched his black eyes move, right to left, right to left, as he scanned through the principal's Arabic script.

When he finally reached the end, he looked up at me, with pride. "It's a great achievement, *habiibti*, to be offered such a position," he said. And I beamed. But then his eyebrows furrowed. "But do you really want to take it?" he asked.

"Yes, of course, Baba," I was quick to reply. "It would be a very nice thing to go back as a teacher, I think. I love the teachers at my school, and I want to be like them; I want to be one of them."

"But don't you want to get married? Have a family? Raise children?"

I hesitated. As I say, in those days, teachers were never married. They were like nuns. So I knew what was coming, and I responded slowly to my father's questions. "Yes," I said. "I want to get married."

"Then you shouldn't become a teacher, Bahiyatii," he said. He knew his words would fall heavily upon me; his pet name for me softened the blow. "If you go back to the school to teach, you will grow up there and grow old there, and you will never be married. You'll become an old maid. It is best for you to refuse the offer." And so I went back for the last part of the year knowing that they would be my very last weeks at the school that I loved.

But even that knowledge didn't prevent the excitement and pride I felt as the academic year came to a close and my graduation was impending. I had spent half a dozen years in that school, and after my initial apprehension those first few days with Rose, I had loved every minute of it. The teachers were so clever and kind and knowledgeable. I had worked hard to earn their respect and admiration as they had so quickly earned mine. And I did earn their respect. I do not think it is wrong for me to be proud of my achievement. Because I was. I still am.

I graduated in 1944 with a teacher's training certificate. Of all the children in my generation from both my parents' families, I was the first to graduate high school. And I was so happy. I was also the only one of my siblings — other than Rose — to have been sent to boarding school. By the time the others were old enough, World War II had begun, and my father couldn't afford the fees. And when the war had ended, the fight for Palestine was already underway. The *nakba* was only four years in the future when I graduated, but we didn't know that then.

My parents and my little brother Sami traveled to Ramallah for my graduation. Sami was six years old. They didn't have the money to stay in a hotel, but my mother had an uncle, Naim, whom she loved, in Ramallah. He was another 'Asfour brother but had not lived with his merchant brothers in the apartment in Shafa 'Amr where my mother had grown up. He had always been fond of his orphaned niece and nephew and had paid for my uncle Aniis's education. So my parents and Sami stayed with *Khalo* Naim and his wife when they came to Ramallah for my graduation.

The ceremony was like a typical American graduation of the time, because it was an American school. There were thirteen of us who graduated together, and I was the top of my class. A few weeks before the big day, the school had arranged for all thirteen of us to travel by bus to Jerusalem to have our class picture taken. It was one of the pictures in the albums that my husband's family saved for me after we fled Haifa. I still have it. The original copy was hung in the Red Hall where the pictures of all the girls who had ever graduated from that school were placed.

For the picture — and for the graduation ceremony — we wore long white dresses. My mother and I had bought and made mine during the previous Easter holiday. We were required to wear petticoats or at least thick slips underneath the skirts so that our underpants wouldn't show. And we were not allowed to wear sleeveless dresses at all.

And though it was forbidden to wear any sort of jewelry at school throughout all the years I spent there, we were allowed to wear simple pieces on the day of our graduation. I had not planned on wearing anything, for I had no jewelry. But the day before the ceremony, my mother pulled me aside and held out a small velvet pouch. I untied the ribbon around its opening and turned it slowly over above my hand. A plain but beautiful gold cross with a fine gold chain tumbled into my palm.

"This is not a gift," my mother told me. "But I will lend you this necklace for now. My uncle Naim gave it to me on my wedding day when I married your father. Wear it tomorrow for your graduation, but keep it and wear it every day after that until you find your husband. Now that you are done with school, I pray you will find a good man to take care of you so that you can raise a family. When you have found him, you can return the necklace to me."

The next morning, I dressed carefully in my dormitory with the other girls and clasped the necklace behind my head, displaying the cross on top of the high neck of my white dress. I held up my head as I received my diploma from Ms. Hannush and the Quaker minister who officiated the ceremony. I caught a glimpse of my parents and Sami in the audience and reveled in their pride.

We were allowed to spend only one more night in our dormitories before leaving the school, so after dinner with my family at *Khalo* Naim's house, I returned to my bed, my school number thirty-eight still posted above it.

The next day, I collected my belongings, my books and clothes and things. I had slept with the necklace my mother had given me around my neck — I thought — but when I glanced into the mirror of the hall on my way out, I didn't see its fine gold chain. I dropped my suitcase and reached my hand up to my chest but found nothing. Running up to the dormitories again, I scoured the area around my bed and cupboard but saw no sign of it. I considered searching the whole grounds, from the dining hall to the assembly where the graduation ceremony had been held, but I knew my parents were waiting for me at *Khalo*'s house, and looking for the necklace would take all day.

I dreaded telling my mother that I had lost her necklace. She would be so angry with me. But I knew I wouldn't be able to keep it a secret for very long; and if I did, when she discovered its loss, she would be even angrier knowing that I had kept it from her. Better to get it over with early on; I would tell her at the first opportunity. But my heart beat with anxiety all the same, and I prayed to God to help me through this ordeal of my own making.

In that part of the world, we don't have lawns or yards. Instead, in front of *Khalo* Naim's home was something like a sidewalk of very fine dirt. And between this lane and the front door was a gate made of iron. I walked to his house, staring at my own feet, weighed down by the loss of the necklace as much as the books and things I carried. As I neared the house, I looked up and my eye was caught briefly by the sun glinting off of something on the edge of the lane, right in front of the gate. I got closer to inspect it and nearly dropped everything in my arms in my shock, for there, lying on the ground in front of my uncle's house, was my mother's necklace, wholly intact, perfectly safe. It must have lain there overnight. I picked it up and tucked it inside the pocket of my skirt. And I whispered a prayer of thanksgiving to God for the miracle he had provided.

THE NECKLACE

A STORY

In those days, people were less suspicious; or maybe it is better to say that they had more faith. Before the betrayals of the colonial powers, before the *nakba*, before the divisions between friends and neighbors that were created, people had more faith — in one another, in the providence of God, in the little miracles of everyday life.

On the day before her graduation from high school, Bahi's mother presented her with a piece of jewelry: it was a gold cross, plain but beautiful, on a fine gold chain. "This is not a gift," Aniiseh told Bahi. "But I will lend you this necklace for now. My uncle Naim gave it to me on my wedding day when I married your father. Wear it tomorrow for your graduation, but keep it and wear it every day after that until you find your husband.... I pray you will find a good man to take care of you so that you can raise a family. When you have found him, you can return the necklace to me."

Bahi took the necklace from her mother and wore it around her neck every day for three years.

On the day that Fariid Owayda came with his parents and his brother to the Habiibi home to ask for Bahi's hand in marriage, he brought with him a wooden box inlaid with iridescent stones and filled — almost so that it wouldn't close — with jewelry. When Bahi's father asked her whether she would accept Fariid's offer, she agreed. And the young man in her father's sala presented her with the box.

After Fariid and his family had left, Aniiseh approached her daughter as she carefully sorted through her fiancé's gifts to her.

"Fariid is a good man," Aniiseh said. "He will care for you well, and you can raise your family with him. And now that you have him and all this jewelry he has given you, you have no need for my necklace. It is time you returned it to me."

Bahi looked up at her mother and smiled as she reached behind her own neck and unclasped the gold chain. She laid the cross gently in her mother's hand. Aniiseh's fingers closed around it, and she carried it away with her.

More than two decades later, Bahi's eldest child, May, had graduated from the American University in Beirut; the campus was just across the street from the apartment in which Bahi, Fariid, and their family lived at the time. A clever, hardworking young woman, May had always succeeded in her academic career, and she graduated with her bachelor's degree with the highest honors.

Bahi was extremely proud of her daughter, and she looked forward to seeing what new heights of success May would achieve in the coming years. But Bahi was worried, too. At twenty-one, May was older than Bahi herself was when she had married Fariid. Of course, times had moved on by then. Bahi wasn't so naive as to misunderstand that. Young women were not expected to get married right away and start having families. May was too well educated for that, anyway. Bahi didn't want her daughter to waste all her talents by becoming a housewife, cooking and cleaning up after a husband and children.

But May showed so little interest in any of it, really, that Bahi was beginning to grow concerned. May had brought home plenty of friends during her years at college — girls and boys — but she hadn't seemed to strike up any special friendships with any of the young men she had met. And even now, when Bahi asked her daughter about the boys in her circle, May just shrugged. "They're all Arabs," she said. "Lebanese, Jordanian, Syrian, some Palestinians, of course."

"Well, what else would they be?" Bahi retorted. "These are the people who send their children to that school. We're all Arabs!"

"Yes, I know, I know," said May. "But the other Arabs don't *think* the way we do, Mama. They behave differently. And all the men think they know things better than I do; they all act the same way, and I don't want to be with someone like that. They don't interest me at all."

So Bahi stopped asking and started worrying — just a little bit.

May began working as a teaching assistant at the university. Before long, she enrolled in classes again — this time as a graduate student, and the closeness she had to her mostly American professors seemed to open a new door in her social life, too. Bahi noticed that among the friends May brought home were fewer and fewer Arabs and more and more European and American citizens, all of them studying or working in Beirut for a finite period of time.

And then May met Bill, a fair-haired American with blue eyes and a confident swagger. On the day Bahi was introduced to him, she said a prayer of thanksgiving to God in her heart. Surely, here was a man May could fall in love with. When May and Bill began dating seriously, Bahi was quick to encourage the romance, convincing Fariid to let the couple enjoy each other's company in the ways common in those more modern days. The two often went out together, without a chaperone, to see films or share dinner, and Bahi would just close her ears against the whisperings of the neighbors and her sisters-in-law. She was insistent that May should be given the opportunity to test out her feelings for this man, to discern whether he might be someone she could settle down with.

And for many months, May's relationship with Bill flourished. Bahi had always been her children's confidante, and she was glad to hear May confess growing feelings for her boyfriend. And then, one day, May reported that Bill was leaving for India.

"India?" Bahi asked. "What is he going to be doing there?"

"I'm not really sure. I mean, his work is sending him there, but he asked them to send him. He wants to go. I think he's figuring a few things out."

"What kinds of things?" Bahi wanted to know. "Will he be gone long? When is he coming back?"

"It's indefinite."

Bahi tried to coax the details out of May, but there didn't seem to be any more. For her part, May was unbothered; it wasn't like she didn't care for Bill, but she wasn't really in love with him either. If he wanted to go to India for a while, let him. May might still be interested in him when — if — he came back, or she might not. She wasn't too concerned.

But Bahi's concern began to grow again with Bill's departure. May was still young, of course. She was only twenty-four. No one, not even Bahi's nosy sisters-in-law, would say May was an old maid — not yet. But if May's feelings for this well-educated, handsome, modern man had fizzled, would she ever find *anyone* who lived up to her expectations?

As May confided in her mother, Bahi confided in her own mother, too. She paid a visit to her parents' house and shared a cup of tea with Aniiseh, telling her of the concerns she had about May, trusting that Aniiseh would know what to do. And she did.

"Don't worry, *ya* Bahi," Aniiseh told her. "I'll come and see May tomorrow and speak with her."

The next day, May was reading in the bedroom she shared with her sisters when she heard her grandmother's voice in the living room. Though her teta and jiddo lived close by in the same neighborhood in Beirut, it was unlike her grandmother to stop by the Owayda home in the middle of the day like this. May put down her book and went into the living room.

"Hi, Teta!" She greeted Aniiseh with a kiss on each cheek as Bahi brought in a cup of tea, set it down on the table, and left the room again.

"Hi, *habiibti*," Aniiseh responded. "Come sit down next to me here. I've brought you something." As May settled herself on the sofa, Aniiseh reached into her handbag and pulled out a small, velvet box. "Here," she said, holding it out to her granddaughter. "Open it."

May carefully picked up the box from Aniiseh's outstretched hand and slowly tilted back the lid. Inside, she found a simple gold cross on a fine, thin chain.

"It's beautiful, Teta," she said. "Thank you. But my birthday has passed. Why give it to me now?"

"This is a very special cross, *habiibti*. My uncle Naim gave it to me on my wedding day when I married your jiddo, and I have kept it ever since. I lent it to your mother on the day she graduated from high school, and she wore it until the day your baba came to our house and asked for her hand in marriage. I want you to wear it now. Wear it and keep it. It's my gift to you. *In shallah*, within the year, it will bring you the blessing of a man who loves you and protects you, a man who will be the best husband for you."

May took the cross out of its box and held it in the palm of her hand, a little bemused smile turning up the corners of her mouth. "Thank you, Teta," she said. "Of course I'll wear it. I don't know whether it will really do what you hope it does, but it will at least look pretty on me!" With that, she unclipped the clasp and draped the chain around her neck.

Not long after that, May attended a party at the home of a well-known American reporter. She had gone with friends, and while there, she was introduced to a young radio journalist named Joe Kamalick, who had recently arrived in Beirut after spending a number of years in Vietnam. At five foot, one inch, May had to tilt her head back almost as far as the lid to the velvet box her grandmother had given her two months earlier to look into Joe's deep brown eyes a foot above her. But the moment she did, she smiled. And Joe responded with a smile of his own, distracted only briefly by the glint of gold he caught out of the corner of his eye as the light hit a small gold cross that lay in the hollow of May's throat.

Leyla Kamalick had come home for spring break. She had left her student days behind her a few years back but had taken up a position as a teaching assistant and Arabic House coordinator at Middlebury College in Vermont and so still enjoyed the holidays of the academic calendar. With nowhere else in particular to go, she had decided to take the week in March to fill up on her mom's Arabic cooking and her dad's bear hugs. Her father, at six foot, three inches, gave hugs that always made her feel safe, even now, as a grown woman.

Of course, it wasn't quite coming "home." Leyla's parents had moved to Washington, DC, a few years ago from Houston, where they had raised their family — two girls, Leyla, the younger one, and Zeyna, her elder sister who was now married and living with her husband not too far from May and Joe. Zeyna's wedding had been a grand affair three and a half years earlier, and Zeyna had just begun to talk with May about planning for a baby. May was excited at the prospect of being a grandmother, a *teta*, finally.

But she worried still a little bit about Leyla. At twenty-five, Leyla was young. Too young for marriage, of course. But May also knew that Leyla hadn't dated anyone seriously since college. And a year ago, she had started the process of ordination to become a priest in the Episcopal Church. May was deeply proud of her daughter's decision and marveled at Leyla's spiritual journey. But once Leyla entered seminary somewhere — which she was bound to do in the fall — and really began to pursue her vocation, how would that affect her romantic life? May had grown up in the church herself and had a very strong faith of her own. She wasn't confused: she knew there was a big difference between an Episcopal priest and a Catholic nun, for goodness' sake. But did *other* people know that difference? Once Leyla started seminary, would there be young men who weren't a bit scared off by her chosen profession?

May worried about these things, but she hesitated to bring it up with Leyla. Her daughter was independent and seemed to bristle anytime May inquired too pointedly about her personal life or offered any kind of motherly advice — about anything really. For all May knew, Leyla wasn't even aware of the potential ramifications of her sense of spiritual calling to her romantic relationships (or lack thereof).

May mulled these things over in her mind as she washed the dishes one evening after dinner, glancing up over the kitchen bar at Leyla and Joe deep in conversation with each other in the living room on the other side of the house. May envied Joe's relationship with their daughter a little bit. Leyla seemed to open up to him in a way she never did with her mother. May wondered whether maybe she could ask Joe to bring the matter up with Leyla, in some subtle way. But she brushed that idea aside as quickly as it arrived. Subtlety was not a gift any of their family members had.

And then, all of a sudden, in a flash of memory between loading two different plates into the dishwasher, May remembered the cross. Teta Aniiseh had given it to her long ago, and she knew exactly where she had kept it. It had traveled with her through the years, from Beirut to Chicago, through two homes in Houston, and finally here.

As soon as the countertops were wiped down, May took off the yellow plastic gloves she wore for that chore, left them drying on the sink, and climbed the stairs to her bedroom. On top of her dresser sat a large wooden box with a flip-top lid on the upper level and a set of three small drawers below. She could picture the cross lying on its fine gold chain in her mind and knew exactly which drawer to open — the middle one.

Sure enough, there it was, tucked back into a corner but still untangled with any other of May's jewelry. She picked it up and laid it across her palm, beautiful in its simplicity.

When she got back downstairs, Joe was in the kitchen rummaging through the liquor cabinet to make himself a drink, and Leyla was tucked up under a blanket on the couch reading a book. Perfect timing.

"Hi, Leylati," May said, crossing the room to sit down next to her daughter. Leyla glanced up and smiled.

"Hi, Mommio," she replied. "Nice dinner."

"Thanks." May paused momentarily. "Can I interrupt your reading for a moment? I have something for you."

"Yeah, sure."

May extended her hand into the space between them and opened it to reveal the cross.

Leyla looked at it and then looked back up at her mom. "That's for me?" she asked, confused.

"Yes. I want you to have it. But just for now. It's not really a gift, more of a loan." Leyla looked even more confused. May continued hurriedly, "It's a family heirloom, really. My grandmother gave it to me, when I was about your age actually. And it's often been given to women in our family. You see, any girl in our family who has worn this necklace has met her husband within the year."

The look of confusion on Leyla's face quickly turned into one of incredulity. She let out a brief, embarrassed laugh. "Mom, you don't believe that, do you?" she asked, smiling. "That can't be true."

"It is too true!" May assured her. "Grandma wore it and met Grandpa; I wore it and met your dad. And it's not just me. It's been passed down or loaned to a number of women in our family, and whoever has it always meets her husband within the year." That last part may have been an exaggeration. May didn't know whether Teta Aniiseh had lent the necklace to anyone else, but it was at least possible. And at this point, a little white lie couldn't hurt. If there was one thing that Leyla was sure to warm to, it was a bit of family history — a nod to the lore that Leyla knew so well from her time with and attention to her grandmother Bahi. And it worked.

"Really?" Leyla asked. May could see she was warming to the idea.

"Really. In fact, you don't even need to wear it every day. The girl just has to have it in her possession; you just put it on from time to time and wait and see. Within the year, you'll meet the man you'll marry."

Leyla laughed again, but simultaneously, she reached out and picked the cross up from May's palm. "This totally sounds like an old wives' tale," she said. "And besides, I'm only twenty-five, Mom! It's not like I'm at risk of becoming an old maid or anything!"

"I know, I know. And I'm not saying you are — or will be. Of course not! But it would be nice to meet someone you could fall in love with, wouldn't it? And really, what harm can it do? Even if I'm wrong and you don't find someone this year, you keep the cross for now and wear it whenever you want to, and whenever you *do* get married, you can give it back to me, so that we can hand it on to the next girl in our family who might want it."

Leyla rolled her eyes only half-jokingly, but May was gratified to see her unclasp the hasp of the chain and buckle it again behind her neck. The cross hung down just below the hollow of her throat, catching the light.

A week later, Leyla received her acceptance letter to a divinity school in Cambridge, Massachusetts, and she began making plans to move that summer.

On her first Sunday in town, Leyla went to worship at the closest Episcopal church, a ten-minute walk from her studio apartment. The ten-fifteen liturgy of Holy Eucharist at Christ Church, Cambridge was fuller than usual since it was the first Sunday of the term and a number of university students and faculty from the numerous nearby institutions were in attendance, on top of the usual Sunday-morning congregation.

Midway through the service, the rector of the church stood at the crossing to make his announcements. He made a point to welcome especially those members of the congregation who were connected with the colleges and universities around the parish and to wish them well on the academic year ahead.

"And before I go on with my announcements," the rector said, "I want to invite the Episcopal chaplain who's here with us today to introduce himself so that all our college folk know who he is. Especially if you're a new student, I really encourage you to meet the Rev. Ben King. He leads a service of Holy Eucharist in the evenings every Sunday at five o'clock. Ben, do you want to come up and tell folks a little bit more about that?"

Hearing the rector's announcement, Leyla wondered whether perhaps the student-focused evening service might be a better place for her to find some community in Cambridge. From her seat on the far left edge of the pew, nearer the back of the church than the front, she strained to see the chaplain and was surprised when he unfolded his long, lean body to stand up at the rector's invitation. He was younger than she thought he would be, maybe in his very early thirties? And he was quite cute. Leyla giggled to herself. Leave it to her to find a *priest* attractive. In a black clerical shirt and a light-weight blazer, the chaplain was so tall that Leyla had no problem getting a good glimpse of him even over the heads of all the people in front of her. He had light brown hair, high cheekbones, big ears, and a wide smile. Definitely cute.

And then he opened up his mouth and began to talk. Leyla had to stifle a squeal. He was British! He sounded quite posh. She decided to stay after the service and introduce herself to him. It was a bit out of character for her; she always felt a little claustrophobic in crowds of people and hated having to navigate them, and the chaplain was sure to be swamped with other new-to-town students eager to meet him, too. But Leyla decided it would be worth it to hear that accent again; and besides, she really *did* want to get more info about that student-centered service.

In the end, she had just a minute or two of conversation with him; he probably wouldn't even remember her if she came to the Eucharist next Sunday evening. But he seemed nice. And he had these lovely little crinkles that appeared on the sides of his eyes when he laughed.

When she got home, Leyla went to her closet; she wanted to change out of the dress she had put on for the service into more comfortable clothing. But as she pulled the dress over her head, the straps caught on something on the back of her neck. She put her arms down and reached behind her. A string of the fabric had tangled with the clasp of the necklace she was wearing. She unclasped the hasp and took off the fine gold chain. That morning, she had thought it was fitting to wear the simple cross her mother had given her to her first church service in Cambridge. But she didn't feel the need to keep it on all day. She smiled and shook her head a little as she laid the necklace carefully in the first drawer of her dresser; her mother was funny in her insistence that the cross would somehow lead her to her future husband.

Beatrice Bahia King was born in the fall of 2014. She was named, in part, after her great-grandmother, still healthy and well at the age of eighty-six. Beatrice's due date was still a week away, but she was clearly eager to arrive; she came out of the womb screaming her independence from the start. The medical staff quickly passed the infant up, past her mother's still-rounded belly, to lie between her breasts for skin-to-skin contact at the hollow of her throat. Beatrice, exhausted by the efforts of birth, quieted somewhat as she listened to the rhythm of Leyla's beating heart.

Ben, standing beside the bed, kissed his wife's tear-filled cheeks and blessed his baby girl.

Ben and Leyla were already parents. Three-and-a-half-year-old Fred was at their home with his teta and pompa, Leyla's mom and dad who had been visiting from Washington, DC, over Thanksgiving. And a few hours after Beatrice's birth, May and Joe brought Fred to meet his new sister. He was enamored. But when the first excitement faded and Fred began to get fretful, the men took him to the hospital cafeteria for a snack. May, Leyla, and baby Beatrice were left by themselves.

May held the infant, wrapped in a light blanket, in her arms as Leyla lay in the bed, her eyes closed. But she wasn't asleep, just resting after a long labor and delivery. When May spoke, Leyla opened her eyes and turned her head toward her mother and her daughter.

"I've brought something for you — and for Beatrice, I suppose," May said.

"Oh?"

"Here, hold her for a minute while I get it out of my purse." She carefully handed the sleeping infant to Leyla. Unzipping the pocket on the side of her bag, May pulled out a small velvet pouch. She untied the ribbon at the opening and, returning to the bedside, poured out the contents into her other hand. Leyla saw the gold cross spill onto her mother's olive-toned palm and chuckled. She recognized it immediately.

"It's a little early for that, don't you think, Mom?" she asked. "Beatrice has only just been born. I don't think she's ready for a husband yet."

"I know!" May replied. "But I figured you should have it and keep it for her, in case I'm not around when the time comes."

"Mom!" Leyla chided. But she was smiling. "Put it back in its little bag, and put it with my things over there. I'll keep track of it for Beatrice — or any other cousin — who might need it in the next generation."

Leyla brought her baby home from the hospital the next day. Ben helped her unpack the suitcase. "There's a little velvet bag here in this side pocket," he told her as she sat on the bed, Beatrice in the bassinet beside her. "Where does it belong?"

"Here, give it to me," Leyla replied. Slowly, she rose from the bed, careful of the pain between her legs. She took the velvet bag from Ben and walked to her dresser on top of which sat a wooden box, inlaid with iridescent stones. The box had been her grandmother's — a gift from her fiancé on the occasion of their engagement. Grandma had told Leyla that the box had been so full of jewelry when Fariid presented it to her that the lid almost didn't close.

It wasn't nearly so full now. It had only a few items of jewelry, plus the clerical collar Leyla always kept in it so it wouldn't get lost in her wardrobe. There was plenty of room for the gold cross on the fine chain in its little velvet bag. Leyla placed it in the box; it certainly seemed to belong there.

And then she heard Beatrice stirring and walked back across the room to her daughter.

BAHI · THE SHINING ONE

Haifa, 1947

In those days, girls didn't speak about love. We didn't tell our fathers, "I don't like him," or "I love this one, not that one." Women were just expected to marry. That's how it was. Women who were still unmarried after twenty or twenty-one years of age were considered old maids. And I did not want to be an old maid. I wanted to find a husband and raise children. But I was only sixteen when I graduated high school. I was fair-haired with green eyes, and I was considered good-looking. But I was not yet ready to be married. So I needed to get a job.

When I returned home to Haifa with my parents after graduation, there was a letter waiting for me from the pastor of the church where the little children went to school. He had written to say that I had been accepted as a teacher at that church school. I had not made an application for that position, but the whole neighborhood knew I had earned my teacher's training certificate, and the pastor of the church and the woman who served as principal of the school wanted me to come work there. It was a good job, I thought, and so I agreed.

They paid me five pounds sterling per month to teach at that school, plus I tutored some of our neighbors' little boys who struggled in their lessons. I earned two pounds per month per boy that I tutored. And all of it, all of the money I earned, I gave straight to my father to help support my family. And my father would give me a little bit of pocket money, but it was never enough for what I wanted, what I needed — stockings and nice dresses and the like. But that's how it was in those days. And I didn't dare say anything about it.

In addition to my paid work, of course, I was also helping my mother in our home, cleaning and cooking and raising my younger siblings. My mother seemed never to stop having more children. While I was teaching and lived at home with my family, she gave birth to her eighth child — another girl — whom they named In'aam. Eight living children and only one of them a boy!

We had always belonged to Saint John's Church since my family first moved to Haifa, and our lives — and the lives of our neighbors — revolved around it. We worshiped there on Sunday mornings. My siblings and I all attended the church school when we were young, the same school in which I taught after my high school graduation. And Rose and I together sang in the choir — the only activity that we participated in that was coed. Which is how I got to know Fariid.

I had always known him, of course. The Owayda family lived in Haifa long before we did. And Fariid's mother's family had been neighbors of my own mother's family in Shafa 'Amr. The Christian families always knew each other. So I had known Fariid since childhood, but I never imagined then that this boy would become my husband one day.

The church choir rehearsed on Friday afternoons, led by Hanna Nucho, to whom my sister Rose was engaged to be married. And we young people loved the choir. All of the youth belonged to the choir, even if you didn't know how to sing. It was like a youth group then. It was one of the few times we were allowed to socialize with each other.

Our church used to put on outings for the choir, picnics and little trips. In the spring of 1947, the church choir had a picnic on the day after Easter. We went to Lake Tiberias, the place where

Jesus walked on the water, and it was a very good picnic. We all brought our lunches with us, and we sat on the grass and ate what we had brought. And without even lifting my head, I knew that Fariid Owayda was looking at me.

Maybe he had noticed me before, for all I knew. Certainly, I had had plenty of suitors in the three years since I had returned home from boarding school. There had been a young man or two who had come to my father, asking for my hand in marriage. But my father wanted us to leave the house in the same order we had arrived to it. He did not want me or one of my younger sisters marrying a man before his eldest, Rose, was married. And I didn't mind. I didn't like any of the men who had tried to be my suitors. They made me feel nauseous.

But by Easter of 1947, Rose was engaged to be married to Hanna, and as I nibbled at my picnic lunch on the shores of Lake Tiberias, and felt Fariid's eyes always on me, something fluttered in my stomach; it wasn't nausea. Out of the corner of my eye, I saw him get up and walk toward the group of friends with whom I was sitting. The fluttering in my stomach intensified; I could feel the blood coursing through my veins, hot but not unpleasant. He sat down beside me, unwrapping the bundle of food he had brought with him.

"Here," he said. "Have some of my lunch; share it with me."

"No, no, thank you," I demurred. "I have enough of my own." If I took food from him, what would that look like? If I accepted even such a small gift from him, what would that say about me?

We sat in silence for a minute, chewing our food. I tried to behave normally, but it felt as though there was a kind of heat between us, and I found the closeness of his body, only half a foot away from my own, distracting.

Finally he spoke again. It was not a whisper, for whispering would have brought more attention to us than normal voices did. But there was something intimate about his tone of voice, something that felt thrilling.

"My family is coming to your house tonight, to visit you and your parents," he said. And I knew exactly what he meant.

"*Ahlan wa sahlan*," I responded. "You are welcome."

As soon as the picnic was over and Rose and I went home, I told my parents, "Fariid Owayda's family is coming over tonight to visit with us." And that's all I had to say. They understood, of course.

The custom in those days was that if you had the family of a young man coming to ask for your hand, the parents of the young woman would tell her to go to the kitchen and make coffee for the guests. So when Fariid came, with his parents and his next-younger brother (Fariid was the eldest of the six Owayda boys), my parents told me to go and make them all coffee. And during my absence, Fariid's father said, "We would like to ask for the hand of your daughter Bahi for our son Fariid."

They waited for me to return to the parlor with the coffee on a tray. And as I walked around the room, offering a cup to each guest in turn, my father spoke to me. "Bahi, *Abu* Fariid and *Im* Fariid are here to ask for your hand in marriage for their son Fariid. What do you say?"

I did not say anything. For it would not be nice for me to show too much eagerness in front of his parents, to jump up and down and say, "Oh yes yes! I want him!" No. It would not be appropriate. But we all knew, in that time, how these things worked. And they all understood my silence for the assent that it was. By not saying anything at all, I was saying yes.

And so I was engaged to Fariid. The Owaydas had come prepared with lavish gifts. Fariid presented them to me: a rectangular box, made of wood, but inlaid with iridescent stones and overflowing with jewelry. All in gold. Earrings and bracelets and necklaces. He loved me so much. He was overjoyed. He couldn't believe his luck that I had accepted to be his bride.

In the next days and weeks, he would come and sit with me in the parlor to talk. Hanna Nucho would come too so that Fariid and I and Rose and her fiancé all spent time together and learned to know and love one another in the first days of the summer of 1947. We didn't know it was the last summer we would see in Haifa.

THE ROMANCE

A STORY

In those days, the country, the society, Palestinians' lives were all about to be thrown into chaos and catastrophe. The signs had been there for years, of course, but most people hadn't really noticed, not yet. As more and more European Jews — fleeing the horrors unfolding across their continent — immigrated to the British mandate of Palestine, the indigenous Arabs (Christian, Muslim, and Jew alike) welcomed them, but tentatively. The newcomers received so much support from the British colonizers: food and housing and stipends. Indeed, they seemed to come to Palestine with a wealth that the Arabs living there couldn't fathom.

But Palestinians didn't pay too much attention — until the rates of immigration seemed to skyrocket. Then the Palestinian elites, the businessmen and clergymen and bureaucrats, spoke to the British authorities and offered some gentle pushback: "Why do these Europeans come to our lands and receive so much from your hands that you've never given to us? Maybe you should slow it down a little. There are complaints." But their concerns fell on deaf ears.

And then, in the waning months of 1947, the signs became unavoidable, no longer ignorable. Tensions between the financially subsidized European immigrants and a band of Arab resisters were building and here and there, first in the countryside and then in the outskirts of villages and towns and finally in neighborhoods of the bigger cities, violence was erupting, like the first bursts of lava from a smoking, grumbling volcano.

Rose Habiibi married Hanna Nucho that summer. And Rose's sister Bahi was planning her own wedding for the new year. Her fiancé, Fariid, was often around Bahi in those months, at her home or sitting next to her at church events or walking beside her along her path in the afternoons as she ran her errands. And since it would never do to be so intimate with one another on their own, they always had chaperones of some kind. Bahi's father or mother were present when the couple met in the Habiibi home, but outside of it, it was more convenient to use their younger siblings as the eyes that would ensure conformity to the courtship customs of the day.

And so it was that Fariid's younger brother Labiib and Bahi's younger sister Abla were also thrown together into each other's company as they tagged along with their older siblings. And how natural, then, that these young people, of similar age and disposition, of similar backgrounds and families, should also fall in love. By the end of the year, through acceptable glances and appropriate comments nonetheless loaded with meaning, the pair had reached an understanding. They were destined for one another and would be next to stand before the altar at Saint John's Church.

On the day of Bahi and Fariid's wedding, Abla and Labiib stood beside the bride and groom as maid of honor and best man, smiling at each other across the bound hands of their sister and brother.

"I will wait until Bahi and Fariid get back from their honeymoon," Labiib thought as he listened to Fariid take the vows of marriage. "As soon as they are back and get settled, Fariid can come with me to the Habiibi home; he shall be the one to ask for Abla's hand in marriage on my behalf."

He would never get the chance. Bahi and Fariid spent ten days in Cairo; when they returned, Bahi's parents were preparing for the departure of their large family. Wadii' had heard too many rumors about women being raped by roving militias of violent Zionists. He had his wife and all those daughters to protect, and Aniiseh was pregnant again with his ninth and final child. There was too much at risk. He would take his family and flee to Cairo, just for a few weeks, maybe a few months, until the British regained control of the situation and the tensions calmed.

As soon as Abla heard of her father's plans, she ran to her older sister, who had just moved into her own apartment as Fariid's wife. She came to Bahi crying. "Please let me stay with you, sister," she pleaded. "I cannot leave with our family now. I know Labiib wants to marry me, and I want to marry him, but Baba is preparing to go to Cairo tomorrow. There is not time for Labiib to ask for my hand. But I must stay here until I am engaged and can marry him. Let me come and live with you and Fariid."

But Bahi couldn't think of it. She loved Abla dearly and wanted her happiness as much as her own. And Labiib was a good man, her husband's brother, certainly worthy of Bahi's favorite sister. But such things were not done. A young woman belonged with her father and must go where he went. It would be scandalous for Abla to stay behind, even in the company of her married sister.

"No, Abla," Bahi told her. "These things are not thought of. You must not speak of them. What would people say? You must go with Mama and Baba to Cairo. *In shallah*, things will work out in the end. I'm sure you'll come back to Haifa soon. Labiib can ask for your hand then."

So Abla left with her father, crying all the time. They would never come back to Haifa.

Months passed; the final stages of the *nakba* took place and culminated with the creation of Israel on May 15, 1948. Sleiman Owayda, his wife Labiibeh, and their sons, except for their eldest Fariid, had clung to their home in Haifa throughout. Sleiman worked as a caretaker for the Anglican mission at the foot of Mount Carmel, a church-run clinic that had long served the community. He felt secure that his relationship with the British would protect his family from the marauders and the violence; and besides, he had no daughters to be concerned about.

But in the early days of the nation-state of Israel, after the surrounding Arab states waged war and lost, the Zionists seemed intent on rooting out even the most well-educated and well-connected Palestinians, like a punishment. At an alarming speed, even in Haifa, even on Mount Carmel where they had cleared their own land to build their lives a generation ago, Palestinian families were violently evicted from their homes to become refugees by the so-called security forces of the new government.

Sleiman still wasn't worried about himself and his wife. His position among the British would keep them safe. But his sons were young men in their own right, even the youngest a teenager. They needed jobs and careers of their own. And they could not be protected by their father's connections any longer. So he called them together and, with a heavy heart, urged them to flee their own home. "Better to leave now — and maybe come back when things are safer — than to suffer humiliation or worse at the hands of those who have stolen so much from us already."

And so the sons of Sleiman began making their plans. The two oldest boys discussed their decision between them. George thought to head to Beirut where their brother Fariid had arrived with his wife. But Labiib urged his brother elsewhere. "Come with me to Cairo, George. Many of our friends and neighbors have already gone there, and I hear there is work to be had. We won't burden Fariid and Bahi, especially not with their child on the way soon." George was persuaded, and Labiib anticipated the day when he would be reunited with Abla.

Indeed, the Owayda boys looked up the Habiibis as soon as they arrived in Cairo and their brother's in-laws offered what hospitality the family could in such circumstances. George and Labiib even spent a few nights in the Habiibi home. They were never left alone with Wadii's daughters, of course, but Labiib nonetheless found a way to communicate his plans to Abla.

"As soon as I can find work and be acceptable to your father, I will ask for your hand in marriage," he promised her.

But there was no work to be found. It seemed as though every Palestinian had heard the same rumors as Labiib had about Egypt and had come seeking positions. A week went by, and then two and then three, and neither George nor Labiib landed a regular job. Finally, word came from their brother Fariid. He had pulled some strings at the company he worked for and secured jobs for his brothers, only not in Cairo, not even in Beirut where Fariid lived, but in Kuwait, whose government had flung open its borders to those displaced by the *nakba*. That's where Palestinian men could get work.

Labiib hated to leave Cairo, hated to leave Abla, but what choice did he have? He could not in good faith ask to marry her when he could not provide for her, and he could not provide for her in Cairo where he would never find work. He would go to Kuwait, establish himself, and earn enough money to prove his worthiness. He would return as soon as possible to marry his love and take her back with him.

But starting anew always takes time, even for a hardworking young man. And life moves forward.

Like any good Christian family, the Habiibis had found a church near their new home in Cairo. There, they met a man who quickly became a friend of the family. Elias the Egyptian, as the Habiibi children called him, was well educated and well mannered. They all agreed he was a very nice man. He would often come to their home for dinner and stay afterward to play cards and socialize with Wadii'. And everyone knew the eventuality of a bachelor's frequent visits to a house full of daughters. One evening, he hinted his intentions to Wadii', praising the fourth Habiibi daughter, Nuha. But Wadii' quickly redirected the young man's attention. As ever, he was insistent: his daughters would leave his home in the same order they had entered it. Abla, Nuha's older sister, should be married first. So Elias the Egyptian asked for Abla's hand in marriage.

Abla did not want him. She did not want to marry an Egyptian, and she had Labiib in the back of her mind, and on her heart. But Labiib was still settling in Kuwait and had not yet come back for her. She dared to tell her father that she would not accept Elias's proposal. But her father was insistent. It was time she was married, and there were no other suitors for her hand.

"You're standing in the way of your other sisters," he told her. "If you don't get married, you will be a stumbling block for them. They can't get married and raise their families until you do."

Not daring to argue further with her father, Abla tried to change his mind through Aniiseh. She spoke with her mother as they worked in the kitchen together. "Elias isn't my only suitor, Mama," she pleaded. "Labiib wants to marry me. We all know he does. He would have asked for my hand already if it wasn't for the *nakba* that happened to us. Ask Baba to give Labiib time to settle in Kuwait, and he will send for me."

"*Laa, laa, laa, habiibti*," her mother replied. "We cannot wait that long. *You* cannot wait that long. And besides, even if he sent for you tomorrow, how would it be for us to put you on a plane to be received by a man? No. These things aren't done. What if you got there and he rejected you and refused to marry you. *Ye ye ye ye ye!* It would bring such shame upon us! What a scandal you would create. And if there is a scandal with one of our daughters, it will taint all your sisters, and we will never get them married to good men."

And so Abla was engaged to Elias the Egyptian. Before the wedding took place, however, the Habiibi family, unstable in their life still lived as refugees in Cairo, moved to Damascus where extended family lived, including Bahi, who had moved there with her husband and young daughter. Abla went with her father; once again it would be unseemly for her to stay behind as a yet-unmarried woman. As Elias prepared to receive his bride into his life and home, the Habiibi family would plan for Abla's wedding in Damascus when Elias came for her.

Throughout the months of her engagement, Abla cried to her sisters. Though Elias had given her a beautiful gold ring to symbolize their betrothal, she refused to wear it, hiding it out of her own sight in a drawer. Whenever her father saw her bare hand, he would demand that she find the ring and put it back on. She obeyed, not daring to refuse her father but crying and grumbling about it the whole time. Frustrated with his weepy daughter, Wadii' would shout at her: "Why do you behave this way? What's wrong with this man? He's very nice."

And Abla explained her feelings. "Number one: I don't love him. And I don't want him. And number two: I don't want to marry an Egyptian. You're all here in Damascus, and I don't want to go back to Egypt and live with this husband and be by myself and alone." But Wadii' would only shake his head and remind her of her duty to her family and her sisters.

For his part, separated from Abla, Elias would write letters and place long-distance telephone calls asking, "When can I come to Damascus and get married?" Despite Abla's lackluster feelings for him, Elias *was* a nice man, as Wadii' believed. He had rented a house and prepared it for his bride in Cairo, purchasing everything she would need to be its mistress: fine linens and expensive appliances and beautiful furniture. He was tired of being a bachelor and Abla was a good-looking woman from a respectable family. He thought they would suit each other well. He had heard the rumors of her earlier desires to marry another man — a Palestinian — but he trusted that God's providence would prevail and Abla would learn to love him as he was learning to love her.

Finally, Wadii' told Elias it was time to come to Damascus. So he did. He took a plane from Cairo, and he and Abla were married the next day. It was a very simple wedding in the church, for Elias had come alone without his family, and the Habiibis had only recently arrived in Damascus themselves. So there was only Wadii' and his family there to witness the marriage. They did not even hand out the traditional candy-coated almonds as favors, for there were no guests to receive them and celebrate. It was just as well, for tears fell slowly down Abla's face throughout the ceremony; she didn't feel much like celebrating.

The couple spent one night at the hotel in Damascus before boarding a plane back to Cairo. During her wedding night, Abla was crying all the time, even in front of her groom. Elias smiled at her, treated her gently and kindly, tried to be as gracious as he could. But it seemed unfair to him, to receive a bride that showed so little happiness in him. It was a hard way to begin their life together, and it planted a seed of suspicion in Elias's heart. Would she ever love him?

When they got back to Cairo, things did not improve. As she had suspected, Abla felt lonely and miserable in the unfamiliar city with a husband she did not love. And nothing Elias had done to prepare his home for her seemed to please her as he had hoped. But in those days, there was nothing to be done. Young people did not marry for love. They married to build a life together and raise a family. And that's what Elias and Abla did. If they argued more than most couples, if they resented each other at times, they did not show it publicly.

In time, though, we become accustomed to even the strangest or hardest circumstances. Abla may not have ever learned to love Elias the Egyptian, but she learned to live with him, to find joy and satisfaction in other aspects of her life, especially in her beloved children. And perhaps hers was the easier path. Elias was never really able to let go of his suspicions of his wife. He knew she would never betray him, but her lack of love for him felt like a betrayal of its own kind. It grieved him greatly. And sometimes grief that is hidden, that is never allowed to be seen, even by its owner, will grow into a dark and monstrous shape.

The months went by and turned to years, which turned slowly into a decade and nearly another. One of Abla's sisters had emigrated with her husband to the United States and told her family that it was a land of plenty. Abla had made her life in Cairo, but it had never been home to her, and the prospect of moving to America seemed tantalizing.

She spoke about it to Elias nonstop. She was sure Elias's company could transfer him to the States. Why not take their children — nearly grown now — and go? But Elias hemmed and hawed and hesitated. "I've heard about those American kids. I've even seen them with my own eyes, the ones who come back with their parents to visit their families here. The teenagers are rude and scandalous. They all smoke and take drugs. I'm sure they have sex with each other!"

But Abla was persistent, and finally Elias relented. His company accepted his application for a transfer, and he moved his family to

New York. Abla got a job working in an office; she was optimistic that, in this new place, not far from her sister, her children with her and nearly grown, her life with Elias would finally feel more joyful, more vibrant. But the move seemed to have the opposite effect on her husband.

The Egyptians have always been a rooted people — farmers and fruit growers long tied to their fertile land. The Lebanese are seafarers, able to adapt to their surroundings and always on the move. And the Palestinians, of course, have been forced to become wanderers, to learn to accept change. But the Egyptians lack such a trait. And none more so than Elias the Egyptian. Now far from *his* land and *his* clan, he felt grief that grew into a kind of misery that neither he nor his family was able to ignore. It would rear up its head in anger or frustration or depression or despondency.

And he began to make dark predictions to Abla, vague at first but eventually quite clear: "One day, you're going to wake up and find me hanging from the ceiling."

Nowadays, there are things that might be done, resources that a husband and wife — or even their teenage children — can grasp hold of, help they can ask for. But then, there was none of these things. And even had there been, what good would it have done? Elias's and Abla's upbringing and culture had taught them to keep such things quiet, to sweep them under the rug, to hide them away for shame. So Elias battled his resentments, and Abla kept her mouth shut.

Until one day, news arrived that another of Abla's sisters was moving to the States. Her husband had gotten a job and would be sent, ahead of his family, for a special training in New York. He would stay with Abla and Elias for the week-long course, and the couple were happy to offer him such hospitality.

Every morning, Abla's brother-in-law would rise early before the rest of the family, make himself coffee and a sandwich, and go downtown for his work. On the fourth day of his stay, he followed his normal routine. The sky was still dark as he groggily shuffled to the kitchen. On his way, he passed through the living room, not bothering to turn on the light. But he didn't need the light to see

Elias already there, in the center of the room, hanging in the darkness from the ceiling by a rope. The terrified houseguest ran to the master bedroom and shook his sister-in-law awake. "Abla! Abla!" His voice was half a whisper, half a scream, laden with urgency. "Abla!" he said again. "*Allah-ynjiinna*. God save us. Abla, wake up! You must come."

Abla woke and heard her brother-in-law's words. She sat up in bed and looked at him in the dim dawn. "He has done it?" she asked. When she repeated it a second time, it was no longer a question. "He has done it," she said, and the weariness and tragedy of her history with Elias the Egyptian weighed down her words.

Once again, the months passed and became years, and the years turned into one decade and then another and another after that. Her children grown and settled with their own families, Abla was retired and living in Houston near to her brother and many of her sisters who had also emigrated and moved to the same area. She loved spending time with them, playing cards with her sisters, gossiping joyfully about their children and grandchildren, preparing Sunday brunches at each other's homes where all the family would gather weekly. She was, finally, happy.

In January of 1998, Abla's sister Bahi marked fifty years of marriage with her husband Fariid, and the couple's daughter May, with help from her siblings, threw her parents a lavish party to celebrate. Bahi's sisters were eager to join in the happy occasion. They bought pretty dresses and new jewelry and offered their help. May asked them to prepare the party favors: half a dozen of the traditional candy-coated Jordan almonds placed into little gauzy white sacks and tied with a golden ribbon. So the sisters made plans to gather at Bahi's house a few days before the event and get the work done.

Bahi and Abla had always been close, separated by less than two years. And Abla knew that Bahi was a rememberer, that she held on to other people's stories as well as her own. So Abla wasn't surprised when, speaking on the phone a few weeks before the party, Bahi gently dropped into their conversation her news.

"All of Fariid's brothers are coming," she said. "All five of them. We can't host them all here, of course, and since the others are coming with their wives, we've offered the invitation to Labiib only. He will stay with us here the whole two weeks of his visit."

So Abla had prepared herself and was ready. When the day came to stuff the party favors with almonds, she stepped through Bahi's front door with a surprising sense of stillness and a deep curiosity. She could hear the voices of a few of her sisters, mingled with Fariid's lower tones and, alongside them, a similar yet distinct male voice. She greeted Bahi and walked into the living room. They were all standing; her other sisters must have arrived just minutes before Abla, for they were still greeting each other with kisses on both cheeks. It gave Abla a chance to see him before he noticed her presence.

He was different. Of course he was. So was she. How many years had it been? He had aged well, though. His hair was white, and his skin was wrinkled and creased, especially around his eyes, but there was still a gentle brightness about him, an innate optimism that exuded from him. "Avuncular," she thought in English. It was a word that didn't really translate into Arabic, a funny sort of word that she surprised herself by even knowing, much less bringing to the surface of her mind.

She knew a bit of his history from Bahi. He had married long ago, only a year or so after her own wedding, a woman he had met in Kuwait. She was extremely attractive. And classy, but in the way of the newly rich whom those early days in Kuwait created. And Abla wasn't sure of the details, but her sense was that it hadn't been an entirely happy marriage. They were living apart now, she knew. Which explained why he was here without his wife. She wondered whether he had learned to live in the marriage as she had done in her own. Or whether, like Elias, he had suffered misery when he lacked the fullness of love.

And then, he was breaking away from greeting her sisters and turning toward her. In the next moment, he would see her. Their eyes locked, and for half a second, Abla felt an intensity of emotion she could not name. Was it fear? Excitement? Anger? Frustration? Grief? Confusion? Perhaps it was all of them combined. But she knew where it ended. In joy. For when he saw Abla, Labiib smiled. And his smile turned to a grin and his grin bubbled into a deep chuckle. He came to her, his arms outstretched. "Abla!" he said as his gentle laughter faded. "How good it is to see you after all these years. You haven't aged a bit!"

She knew it for the lie that it was, but she thanked him anyway, kissing him on both cheeks as they briefly embraced. It was good to see him, too. So very good.

On the night of Fariid and Bahi's anniversary party, Labiib and Abla danced together, over and over. And the next day, a Sunday, each one stood beside their sibling — just as they had fifty years ago — as the couple renewed their vows to one another in their church. Abla glanced down the space between the priest and Bahi and Fariid as the former wrapped his stole around the couple's joined hands and said the blessing. And Abla saw Labiib looking back at her. And they smiled.

BAHI · THE SHINING ONE

Haifa, 1948

In those days, during the invasion of Palestine, the country was in total turmoil. But well before then, for years, even when I was still a schoolgirl, the British authorities who controlled my country had been importing European Jews into our cities and towns. They settled and lived among us peacefully at first, but in the months before my wedding, all of that had changed.

By then, the Zionists had arranged themselves into "militias" — that's what they called themselves, what the British authorities called them. The European Jewish men formed up into armed groups — weapons seemed to be everywhere by then, so easy to come by if you knew the right people, were on the "right" side — and roamed the streets, outside of shops, inside our neighborhoods. "Militias" they were called, patrolling to protect the new Jewish immigrants; but they didn't feel like militias to us. They felt like terrorists. And who were they protecting the Europeans from? From us? From our friends and neighbors who had always lived here, who had always called Haifa our home? It confused and disconcerted us.

And then there were the shootings. The men in these militias would shoot, and we never knew the reasons why. Sometimes whomever they shot at was hit; sometimes whomever they shot at was killed. And nothing was ever done about it. The British security forces were supposed to be keeping the peace, but they didn't seem to care. And so there were some who figured it was time to take matters into their own hands. These Arabs formed militias of their own, and word spread quickly: our loyalty lay with our own people; if you valued your life, you would not cooperate with the Zionist invaders. Even those immigrants with whom we had formed the beginning of friendship were cut off from us. Non-Arabs — whether British or Jew — were not to be trusted.

In the midst of these times, I married Fariid. We were married on January 3, 1948, in Haifa. By that time, most of the Arabs' shops were closed because of the conflict, and some of the merchants had already fled the country. In the Jewish quarters, the shops were open, and trade was happening, but if a Palestinian was seen buying things from the European Jews' ready-made clothing shops, he was immediately shot by the revolutionaries — the Arabs who were resisting the invasion.

We could buy only the material for my wedding dress, and there was a seamstress who came to our house to make it. But I borrowed everything else from friends and from my sister Rose, who had been married the previous summer — the veil, the gloves, the bouquet, everything — because there was nowhere to buy them. We had printed invitations for the wedding ceremony, but we were not able to send them because there was no post, and we could not deliver them by hand. We had to steal ourselves to the church for the ceremony, and although the church was meant to be full, only my family and Fariid's family were there. When we left the church, no one sang the celebratory blessings, the lulus that announced our joy and heralded a bright future. Even the photographer never showed up. I never had any pictures taken. The only pictures I have were taken when we came back from our honeymoon. I was already pregnant by then.

It was raining on our wedding day. The gray light shone valiantly through the windows of the church. With his long white stole, the minister bound my hand together with Fariid's and blessed our marriage in the eyes of God. And then Fariid lifted my veil and kissed me chastely on the cheeks. And so it was done.

We went to Cairo for our honeymoon. It was another world compared to what we had just left behind. Cairo had shopping malls with escalators and elevators, beautiful theaters, electric streetcars. We didn't have anything like it in Palestine. And best of all, amid the hustle and bustle of the streets, Cairo had peace. There was no undertone of constant fear, no sounds of unexpected explosions, no fighters — plain-clothed or uniformed — roaming the streets.

We spent ten blissful days in Cairo, and then we went back to Palestine to begin our life together.

But we were naive and inexperienced. By those days' standards we were educated, but by these days' standards we were ignorant. We knew nothing. And we would find ourselves thrown into a wide, deep ocean, and we would have to fight our way out.

We came back by train from Cairo to Haifa. It was our first experience in first-class train cars. Everything was luxurious: linens, tablecloths, waiters, very good food. We felt like kings. We couldn't wait to tell both our families about our experience. But as soon as we got to the station, there was no one to meet us but the British security forces. At the time, the Zionist terrorists used to put explosives in big barrels and roll them into the Arab quarters of the town. The British instated curfews to try to calm things down, curfews that sometimes lasted for days, even a week or more. You were not allowed out of your home: if no one was on the street, no one could kill or be killed.

So when Fariid and I got back from our honeymoon, the British authorities told us there was a curfew in the city, and any civilian on the streets might be shot. Fariid and I could not go home. Instead, two policemen took us in their car to a quarantine. There was no other place to stay that night.

I remember that the food there was awful. There was only stale bread and water, and even the water tasted bad. When I asked one of the authorities about it, he said, "What do you think, that you're in a luxury hotel? You should be thankful for what you're getting." So I kept my mouth closed after that.

The place was segregated, women separated from the men. Husband separated from wife. So they put me in one small cold room, like a jail cell, and Fariid in another even though there was no one else in the quarantine. I was scared they would try to rape me, so I didn't sleep. The following morning, the curfew was still on. Fariid called his brother, George, who worked for the Haifa municipality, and George called someone who was in charge of the fire brigade, who sent one of the fire engines to the quarantine to take us home. It was a long way from the quarantine to where we lived on Mount Carmel, but the sirens were ringing the whole way. No one would shoot at a fire engine with sirens blaring.

We got to Mount Carmel safely, but the whole way we were scared. We clung to each other in our uncertainty, our hands bound as tightly together as when we had stood at the church's altar just a few weeks before.

When we arrived home, we did not have the energy to tell our families about our trip. We went to Fariid's parents' house where we had dinner, and we spent the night there, because it had already gotten dark. The next morning, the curfew lifted, so Fariid dropped me off at our new apartment nearby and went to work. He worked in the offices of a British company called Spinneys that supplied shops with food and fish and meat. When he left for work, I was scared that he would not come back. I knew that, as a Christian, working for the British, he might be killed by the mostly Muslim Arab revolutionaries, and as a Palestinian he might be killed by Zionists. So every day, I feared for his life.

We arrived back from our honeymoon in mid-January, and from then on, there was no peace. All the time, all the time, we used to hear shootings and explosions. At night I would lie in the bed next to my husband's bed, and we would wake up every few hours, hearing the tat-tat-tat of gunfire somewhere in the neighborhood or the mortars landing nearby. In some ways, we grew accustomed to it; in some ways, it seemed always a threat.

Sometimes there was bread and meat and vegetables, and sometimes not. Food began to get scarce. There was no communication between cities. No telephones, no buses, no cars, no taxis, no nothing. Homes were invaded, men killed, girls and women raped. We learned of it through rumor, word of mouth from the cousin of our neighbor's brother-in-law or from the nephew of my mother's housemaid. *Hajjii Mahmoud was killed by the Zionist invaders. Abu Kariim was taken from his home by the British security, and we don't know why — or where he is.* And the British whom we knew whispered to us to leave, that it wasn't safe, that worse was to come.

My father took my mother (pregnant with my last sister) and siblings and left for Egypt. I was married and newly pregnant with my own first child, so I stayed behind with my husband. But the whole time, rumors swirled, curfews and conflict worsened, and the British and the Zionists put greater and greater pressure on us to leave. Eventually, there was a mass exodus. Everybody we knew left, aside from Fariid's family. When my husband went to work, I was left alone in the whole apartment building.

In the end, we did not decide to leave so much as we fled. The attacks became too frequent; the threats Fariid received became too explicit. Leave or be killed — or worse. Still, we thought we would come back in a couple of weeks when the conflict died down. We did not pack much. We left with the clothes on our backs and one suitcase between us that Fariid was able to carry. I wore a dress and a coat and one pair of shoes, and I packed a few other items of clothing. I left everything else except my jewelry — my gold bracelets and my watch and my rings. My father-in-law said, "If you don't come back, we don't want you to lose your jewelry. If your husband can't find a job, you can sell this jewelry and live." There was a ship taking everyone who was fleeing from Haifa at the seaport. And so Fariid and I fled to Lebanon by a coal-powered cargo boat operated by the Spinneys company. It was mid-April, and I was twenty years old.

A girl of twenty in those days was like a girl of ten now. I was naive. I was scared. With us on the boat was a mixture of peasants and workers, and I did not talk to any of them, because I didn't know who was safe or appropriate for me to talk to. Fariid and I were trying to focus on what to do now and what to do next.

The ship was overloaded with people. Spinneys used it to transport goods, even cars and trucks. But that day, people flocked to the ship, as though they were being herded away from Haifa to Beirut. There was no food, and Fariid and I had eaten only a small breakfast. The trip took two days and one night. I was pregnant with my daughter, and I was seasick. Hungry and nauseous, all the time. I remember that Fariid had given me an expensive bottle of perfume that was in my purse, and when I opened my purse to get a handkerchief, I smelled the perfume and got so sick I threw it into the sea.

It was also very cold. At night, I started shivering. So Fariid went to find out whether there was room for us downstairs. He told them his wife was pregnant and cold, and so they made space for us to sit. I still wonder how I didn't lose the baby.

The owners of the ship had tried to make space for more people by creating an extra steerage compartment. They had loaded thick wooden boards and placed them in between the deck and the steerage floor, which resulted in a makeshift second floor. We were sitting beneath these boards, but we didn't know the ceiling was made of boards that were mobile. We thought this was the ceiling of the ship. As soon as we sat down and got settled, one of these boards fell from above us, and a woman fell through the space. Fariid was struck on the head by the board, and the woman fell on top of him.

I thought my husband was going to die, and I wondered, "What am I going to do amid all these strangers?" I knew no one on the boat, and I knew no one in Beirut except my sister Rose and her husband, Hanna, but I didn't know their address or their telephone number. I depended on my husband. This is how it was.

Fariid told me later that there was only darkness when the board hit him. They started pouring buckets of water on his head. There was no blood that we could see, but he wasn't moving. And I thought to myself, "If he dies, what will happen to me?"

After a while — it must have been only minutes, but it seemed a lifetime — Fariid woke up and seemed to be all right. I thanked

God for that small mercy, but I was still so very scared. And I prayed silently to myself all through the trip, "Please, God, help me. Do something about this." But I did not have the same relationship with God I have now. I was a Christian and went to church, but I did not know God as well as I would grow to know him later in life. I learned Scriptures and sang hymns, but it was not enough, because danger was glaring at us, and we could not face it.

When the boat landed in Beirut, there were no ladders for people to get off the boat. It landed on the dock, and the ship was higher than the pavement by about five feet. So Fariid went down and held his arms up. I held his hands and I jumped. It seems unimaginable to me now. How did I not lose the baby?

The Lebanese authorities met everyone and told us that we must go to the refugee camps. Fariid said, "I'm not a refugee. I am here in charge of the cargo for Spinneys Ltd." He showed them his identification papers, so they let us go. We went to the offices of Spinneys, and as soon as we got there, we told them we were hungry and we'd pay anything for a sandwich. They brought us sandwiches and juice and fruits and vegetables. They stuffed French bread with butter and cold cuts and cheese. Each of us ate two of those sandwiches. I was dead from hunger. Two days and one night with no food.

After that, we went to Rose and Hanna's house. We stayed with them temporarily. My sister Rose was excited to see us because she had been lonely living in Beirut with no family, no friends. She was pregnant herself — much more heavily pregnant than me. And she delivered her baby while we were living with them, her first child, a boy, and they named him Nicola and called him Nino for short.

I helped her with Nino as much as I could in the early days, but caring for Rose's baby made me anxious for my own. How would I care for a child in this strange place? I longed to go back and have my baby in my house in Haifa, among my family and my neighbors. But the other refugees who came told us not to go back because the authorities would not let us back in.

Eventually, Fariid rented an apartment on the top floor of a building, but it was poor quality, because the owner built it quickly in order to house refugees. Just walls and a ceiling that leaked all the time. There was no gas, no appliances, so we bought two kerosene cookers that I hated using. We bought temporary couches that we sat on during the day and slept on during the night. We bought all our necessities, but everything was cheap quality, because we thought we'd be going back.

A few weeks later, two of my brothers-in-law came from Palestine, evicted from their home after the *nakba*, and they stayed with us, because they had no other place to go. We lived like that for months, my husband and his brothers and I, in our small, leaking, dingy rooms at the top of a building in Beirut. It was not my home.

And in that place, in that time, I gave birth to my baby girl. I was only a girl of twenty myself, inexperienced, naive. We named the baby "May," because, in Arabic, it is a name for Mary. The name was not very common, and it was pretty. Plus, it would work in both Arabic and English, and I imagined that one day she would maybe go to the States.

But at the time, it was all just a fantasy; the reality was so much harsher. I was a young mother; I had a new baby; I had my brothers-in-law living with me; I had a new husband and a run-down house that could never be my home. My baby was crying all the time, because I did not know how to care for her. And I knew no one who could help me. Anytime I started breastfeeding her, I would fall asleep. I cried almost all day, because I was tired and poor. But I cried to myself only. I cried silently to myself. I did not let any of them — even my own husband — see me cry.

BAHI · THE SHINING ONE

Beirut, 1948

In those days, the Lebanese hated the Palestinians. In some ways, I can't blame them. We came as refugees to Lebanon, and it must have felt to them as though they were living in a small house and barely had enough for themselves when we came, and we were even poorer than them. And we needed so much. We were refugees.

My husband continued to work for a short period of time with the company he worked for in Palestine, Spinneys. But all the other employees were Lebanese, and Fariid, of course, was Palestinian. And they didn't like that he was given a job with them, even though he had worked for the same company in Palestine. So they came together against him and whispered about him behind his back. And in the end, we were refugees; Fariid did not have a work permit. So he was asked to leave.

And I was so scared. I was afraid we would starve; I had a little baby. Neither I nor my husband had IDs; we had no work permits.

But both Fariid and I loved to read. And when he was working, Fariid met a man who was a customer at Spinneys, named Mr. Alamadiin. Mr. Alamadiin was a businessman and entrepreneur from a very well-to-do Lebanese Druze family. When we knew him, he was in the process of beginning a new airline company in Lebanon. My husband's family are sociable people — none more so than Fariid. Whenever Mr. Alamadiin came into Spinneys to shop, Fariid would engage him in conversation. Though Mr. Alamadiin was Lebanese, too, he was friendly with Fariid; he did not look down upon us. And the two men discovered they had much in common. For one, they both loved cowboy books — fiction books about the American Wild West.

When Mr. Alamadiin heard that Fariid was being let go from Spinneys, he invited him to work for his new project, starting an airline company. Fariid was a fast typist, and he could do figures; he was always good at math. So Fariid accepted the job.

Mr. Alamadiin was a very good boss. He had been educated in the States, and we used to say that he was "content and not hungry." That is what we say, in our culture; it is an idiom by which we mean that someone isn't after money, that he isn't greedy. And that's what Mr. Alamadiin was like. He was content and not hungry. So Fariid was well paid. He started out as Mr. Alamadiin's secretary, but he was quickly promoted, and he brought home a good check that allowed us to live comfortably even though we always had a lot of house guests: Fariid's brother stayed with us for months, and others came from Palestine. If they didn't have anywhere else to go — and most of them didn't — we would offer them hospitality for a night or two, sometimes as long as a week, until they found some shelter of their own.

So I wasn't scared that we would starve anymore. In fact, after that first awful boat trip to Lebanon, we were never hungry. Food was plentiful. Fariid used to buy a lot of meat, vegetables, fruits, everything. That is how the Palestinians are. We like to eat. It is the custom that every family should have a lot of food at their house, because this is a sign of being "content and not hungry."

In those days, fruits and vegetables had seasons — like oranges and cabbages in the wintertime, grapes and watermelons in the summer. Fariid was always the first to buy these things when they came to market. No one else would bring oranges home at the very beginning of its season, because they were still expensive, but Fariid would bring them. He loved buying the first fruits and the first vegetables of the season to bring home to me. And everybody would eat and would be content — the whole household.

Mr. Alamadiin was very happy with Fariid, and he wanted to keep Fariid with him permanently as he was building his fledgling company. So Mr. Alamadiin was working to get Fariid the proper paperwork he needed to stay in Lebanon, even as a Palestinian refugee. Fariid needed a Lebanese ID and a work permit. But the bureaucratic system in Lebanon is known for its red tape, especially when it came to Palestinians, and there was a lot of uncertainty about whether it would be possible. Until then, Fariid was technically working illegally, and we didn't like that. It was a precarious position to be in.

In the meantime, we heard that the Syrian authorities were giving work permits, legal protections, and Syrian IDs to all Palestinians. Plus, my father had a brother, my uncle Adiib, who had fled to Damascus and established a life there, so we wouldn't be alone.

So we thought, "Let's go to Syria, where we can at least get IDs, where we can build a future with more certainty." I don't know whether it was the right decision. But we were naive; we had been tossed into a deep sea by the people who had taken our home from us. We were just trying to survive, to keep from drowning. And whenever we saw an opportunity for stability, it was like finding an island in the midst of the deep sea, and we went toward it. If Fariid had stayed in Beirut with Mr. Alamadiin, perhaps we would have gotten very wealthy, for the company he built was successful, and Fariid had been with him at the beginning of it. But all we wanted then was security, certainty, a chance to stop and rest after being tossed by so many violent waves.

So we took our baby girl and went to Damascus. Once again, we left everything behind. We took a taxi from Beirut, and we carried with us only one suitcase each, and May's crib, which we fit into the trunk of the taxi. Everything else we left behind with Fariid's brother, who remained in that small, dingy apartment on the roof of a building there.

The border we crossed between Lebanon and Syria was on top of a mountain, and there was so much snow that it made walls on either side of the taxi as it drove us into the new country. The snow piled up three or four times higher than the car we rode in, like the water walls of the Red Sea when the Israelites escaped slavery in Egypt.

And it was cold. So cold. It seems like every time we moved, every time we left one place for another, I nearly froze to death. There was no heat in the taxi, and my baby and I both got chilblains; I remember holding May's hands in my own, trying to keep them warm. Both of us nearly froze to death, our fingers and toes turning red and swollen. It was January of 1949. May was four months old.

When we arrived in Damascus, we went to my uncle Adiib's house and spent our first few nights there until Fariid found us an apartment. Once again, the apartment was on the top floor of a building; it was very hot in summer and very, very cold in the winter. Our first morning, I went to turn on the tap in the kitchen to make our coffee and tea, but no water came out. In that time, there was plumbing, there was water in the taps, but it wasn't modern like today. All the water for the building was kept in a reservoir on the roof; it wasn't insulated. And it was so cold that the water in the reservoir had frozen, and it would not flow into our house. So Fariid went out in the cold to the reservoir where the water was kept and broke the ice with a hammer. He put chunks of it into a bucket and brought it back to the apartment, and I had to heat it up over the kerosene stove to make our coffee and tea that day.

My uncle had helped secure a job for Fariid in Damascus working for Mobil, the oil company. At first it was a simple low-level office job. But Fariid was always a hard worker; he quickly proved himself and got promoted. He always made sure I was provided for. Even when we had to start over in new places, even when things were hard.

Not long after we moved to Damascus, my father brought my family there. They had never settled in Cairo where they fled during the *nakba*, and they, too, took advantage of Syria's open-door policy to Palestinians. So I was reunited with my sisters — one of whom, my last sister, Elham, I had not yet met. She had been born in Egypt, just a few days after my own baby, May. My sister and my daughter would grow up together, like cousins, like sisters themselves.

As soon as they arrived in Damascus, my parents came to Fariid and asked him to move to a new place with them. They wanted us to move to a big house, all of us together, so that we could share expenses and share experiences. In my heart of hearts, I didn't want to. I thought, "I am married to Fariid, and I want to live with Fariid, not with all my family and my siblings." But my father didn't have a job then; he was providing for his whole family just from his pension, and it wasn't enough. So they thought if we moved in together, it would be better. Fariid agreed. He did it for me, in the end, because he wanted to help my family, to provide for them.

So we moved to a very nice house that had a big back garden with a fountain and jasmine trees. And I lived with my family — with my husband and my daughter, my parents and my sisters and my brother. And I got pregnant again, with my second child, and delivered him then, when we were still living with my family in that big house.

We named him Sleiman, after his father's father, as was the custom then — as it still is today in that part of the world.

One day, Fariid came home and took me aside, away from the listening ears of my sisters, and told me he had received an unexpected phone call at his work. We did not have phones in our homes in those days, just in the office buildings and workplaces. And one of my fellow graduates from the Friends School in Palestine had found the number of Fariid's office and called him there. She said that she herself had heard from one Mr. Foley, who was a teacher at that school now and was recruiting graduates of the Friends School — men and women both — to give them scholarships for more education in the States. My old classmate remembered me and how well I had done in school and suggested my name to this Mr. Foley.

I was so excited. Fariid and I discussed it, and we both thought it was a good idea. We wanted to know more. So Mr. Foley came to visit us in Damascus, and we met with him and talked about it. They would send me and my family — my husband and my children — to the States, and we would live there in this program, which was created specifically for Christian Palestinians. And I would receive more schooling, and Fariid could have a work permit and find a job. I thought it was a dream come true. And Fariid needed little convincing. He was enthusiastic about the plan. We thought we would go to the States together and live as a family.

But then we spoke about it with *my* family. The same evening after we met Mr. Foley, we told my parents the good news. We thought they would be happy for us and would encourage us. But that is not how they reacted. "*Ye ye ye!*" my mother shrieked. "*Laysh?!* Why? Why would you want to do such a thing? Go overseas to a strange country where *you* will be the strangers? Where you know no one, where you have no family, where you would be all alone by yourselves?" My father, too, counseled us against it, though more calmly. It was foolish, he said, to leave the certainty and stability we had finally established for ourselves here, for an opportunity where the outcomes were entirely unknown.

We thought about it, and we thought, then, that my parents were right. Fariid had a good job where we were; our children were well provided for; we were surrounded by our family and our church and our neighbors. So we stayed there; we stayed with what we knew.

Fariid called Mr. Foley. Mr. Foley said he understood, but he told us if we ever changed our minds, if we ever decided to go, we could just call him at the Quaker headquarters. Just call him, and we could go to the States. I think now of that opportunity that we refused, and I wonder what would have been different if we had taken it. But then, we didn't know how to take such a chance, to risk instability and insecurity again. Still, after that, I always had it in my mind that one day we *would* go to the States and live there. I dreamed about it often, even as I learned to be happy where I was.

THE FALL

A STORY

In those days, the early days of Israel's existence, there were lots of people who took advantage of the situation, of the people who were displaced, of the destruction of families by the Zionist invaders who tore us apart.

So many of the Palestinian refugees fled to Beirut and to other places of Lebanon that there came to be a kind of underground railroad, "agents," they were called, who would take Palestinians still living in Palestine — now called Israel — to see their families in Lebanon even though they didn't have IDs. For a very high price, these agents would ensure that the Palestinians could make it to Lebanon safely and then be able to cross the border to get back home.

In the last month of 1951, Labiibeh longed to see her sons who were living in Beirut. And she decided to use the agents who began operating almost immediately after the *nakba* to transport Palestinians illegally in this way and were still at work three years later. She knew of the high cost, but the Owayda family was wealthy enough; their lives and livelihoods had been protected by their position on the English mission.

Labiibeh was adamant that she would be with her sons for Christmas Day. Her husband Sleiman wouldn't hear of it. He did not think it was safe to travel like that. But Labiibeh was not submissive like other Arab women. She insisted she would go. They argued about it in the early weeks of that December, back and forth, back and forth.

"I won't let you go to Beirut with these corrupt men, Labiibeh. It's not safe. It's not right."

"I don't care what you think. I will be with my sons for Christmas. It is not right for a mother to be without any of her children during this holy day. We have the money for it. I want to go."

"No. You mustn't. You must stay with me on the mission. We will stay here and fulfill our duty to our place here, to the people here."

"I will stay until the day before Christmas, but on Christmas Eve I am going to go to Beirut to be with my children."

"*Ya* Labiibeh. I won't hear of it. I will prevent you from leaving. I won't let you go."

"You cannot stop me."

And so, against her husband's wishes, Labiibeh made the arrangements. She found the name of one of the agents and began making her plans.

The day before her departure, two days before Christmas, Labiibeh walked downtown to the Haifa city center, to meet the agent who would take her to Beirut the next day. She was there to pay him the money he demanded for the trip. She had taken with her, in her purse, all the cash that was required, and she met the man, paid him, received her receipt, and confirmed the details of the travel. And then she walked back home.

The English mission for which Sleiman worked and where they had always lived was near the foot of Mount Carmel, on one of the lower terraces of the mountain. To get from one terrace to the next, she had to climb a set of outdoor stairs, and that's what she was doing, climbing the last staircase to her home, when one of her neighbors spied her from a window of a nearby building.

Labiibeh paused in her climb when she heard her name being yelled: "Labiibeh! Labiibeh!" She lifted her head and saw her neighbor leaning out the window. She began to raise her hand in greeting to the woman, but before she could get any words out, the lady cried out again. "Labiibeh! Labiibeh!" she screamed. "Hurry home! Your husband has died!"

Labiibeh ran as fast as she could up the rest of the stairs to meet her neighbor. "What do you mean?!" she asked urgently. "What do you mean my husband has died?!"

The story poured quickly out of the neighbor who was both horrified by and eager to be the first to share the news with Sleiman's now widow. Sleiman had climbed a pine tree in one of the many orchards that belonged to the mission. He was trying to cut down one of the big branches to serve as a Christmas tree for the upcoming holiday. At fifty-two years of age, Sleiman was not young, but he was hearty and healthy and had always taken on this task in the days before Christmas every year before.

High up in the branches of the tree, Sleiman had lost his footing, slipped, and fallen to the ground. When they found him, they said he must have fallen on his ear, "the killing place" of the body, for blood was pouring from his ears, his mouth, and his nose. The doctors of the mission were called to his side, but by that time, there was nothing they could do.

Labiibeh cried and cried. Her grief was frantic. Finally, as the initial shock turned into more measured sobs, Labiibeh spoke through her tears. "He told me," she said to her neighbor. "He told me he would prevent me from going to Beirut. And now he has."

None of her sons would make it to their father's funeral. They did not have the paperwork to cross over the border into the land that was their home.

BAHI · THE SHINING ONE

Damascus, 1952

In those days, we didn't know what we were doing. Not really. We were well educated and well read, and we were grown; we had our own family. But we were naive. I was so naive. I didn't know anything really.

We lived for a little more than a year in the house in Damascus with my family. But I wasn't entirely happy there. Perhaps it's not right, not Christian for me to say it, to think it, but I confess that I didn't want to serve anyone except my own husband and children. And because we lived all together, I ended up doing so much of the housework to serve other people. I did all the laundry and the dishwashing, not just for Fariid and May and Sleiman but for my parents and my siblings, too. And I didn't like it.

And Fariid was earning good money, and my family was getting some income, so we decided to rent our own homes, separate from each other. And I was glad about that.

By that time, Sleiman — my first Sleiman — had been born, and we were happy because we had one girl and one boy. And we had settled down. Fariid had bought furniture — good furniture this time, not temporary, poor-quality things — and we had good clothes and plenty to eat. And our apartment was very nice; we no longer froze to death in the winter or baked in the summer. I was living with my two children and my husband, with my family close by but not on top of us.

I felt that, finally, I was able to really enjoy my life as a wife and a mother. And I loved my children. When we moved to that apartment on our own, May was four years old, and Sleiman had just turned one. I was very proud of them. Because I was a teacher, I was raising them to be learners, even at their young ages. I was teaching May to read, and we enrolled her in a little school down the road. She was very smart, very clever.

And Sleiman! Unlike my experience with May, when I suffered such hardship, with Sleiman, I was able to really enjoy his babyhood, to attend to his development and growth, because I didn't have to worry about leaking roofs and cold apartments and lost jobs. Plus, Sleiman was such a good-tempered baby, even in his early infancy. He slept well and ate well. And by the time we moved into the new apartment, he was beginning to take his first steps. He was chubby and smiley and so sweet. Fariid and May and I all liked to watch him toddle around; he made us laugh with joy. Soon, he even began to say a few words, and I loved him very much. At that time, I thought I had everything I ever wanted in life, right there, under that roof. And I was so happy.

I was still a reader – I would always be a reader. We got magazines from England and the States that I would read in my spare time. I liked to do these things, to learn what life was like in that part of the world, and I still dreamed sometimes that we would go there, to the States one day. I got *Parents* magazine and *Time* and *Reader's Digest*.

Fava beans were plentiful in Syria in those days. People there used them in a lot of their cooking: mashed with oil and salt for breakfast, in lunch and dinner dishes with yogurt and rice or meat. And I didn't make them often for my family – they were not a food we had cooked much with in Palestine – but because they were very accessible, very easy to come by, every once in a while I did.

Once, I decided to use them in the dinner I was planning for that evening, so I sat down in the kitchen to prepare them – to shell them and clean them. Fariid was at work; May was at her school; and Sleiman was toddling around me, playing. He came over to me where I sat and held out his hand, and I just gave him two or three of the beans. I thought he would play with them. And he did, for a minute or two. And then, he put them in his mouth and ate them.

His reaction was almost immediate. Very quickly, he started crying — not really crying out loud but whimpering, holding his tummy. And I could see in his eyes and by the tightness of his body that he was in pain. So I stopped my work, and I picked him up and carried him and cuddled him and tried to comfort him. But he was not comforted.

Finally, I decided to try feeding him his lunch, the food I had set aside for him that day. I thought maybe he was hungry and if I fed him, he would eat and fall asleep for his nap and wake up feeling better. So I set him down at the table and gave him his food, but he refused to eat it. And he was still whimpering the whole time.

And that was when I noticed his skin. He was turning yellow. It happened so quickly. Right before my eyes, I could see his skin take on this sickly yellow hue. And beneath that, I could see his veins, all along his body. It was like someone had given him poison. And I realized that that person was me.

All of a sudden, I remembered reading an article in *Parents* magazine some months earlier. The article said that some Mediterranean children suffered from a disease that made them very sick when they ate fava beans. This lack of tolerance for fava beans was passed to them from their mothers, though it affected only little boys, not girls. But it was only one article in one issue of one of my magazines, and I hadn't thought much of it at the time. I had thought, "We don't eat fava beans very much. And anyway, this wouldn't ever happen to us."

But now, I looked at my baby, my Sleiman, and I remembered. And I realized I had given my own son this poison.

About that time, Fariid came home from his work for his afternoon meal. Panicked, I explained what was happening to Sleiman. Fariid took one look at him and decided to take him to the doctor.

So we did. But the doctor told us to go straight to the hospital with him. When we got there, the hospital doctor saw us and examined Sleiman, who was clearly miserable by then. His skin was still yellow but very, very pale, and as I held him in my arms, I could feel and hear his heart beating so fast. I knew it wasn't right; it wasn't normal. And he was crying still, but he was so weak, it was more like a low moan. I clung to him, holding him to my chest as we spoke with the doctor.

"Earlier this morning, I gave him a few fava beans," I told the man. "But just one or two. He barely ate any." Surely just a few small beans couldn't be the cause of such suffering, I thought.

The doctor looked at me, and I saw the pity in his eyes.

Fava bean poisoning. That's what they called it. Sleiman's red blood cells were turning into white ones, they said. They would try to give him a blood transfusion, but they were afraid it was too late. They didn't think it would work.

They were right. It didn't work.

I don't like to remember these things.

I don't remember the day that Sleiman died. But I remember that it was late in the springtime, almost summer. I remember wondering how the earth could be warming so wonderfully after the bitter winter when I still felt so incredibly cold. As though my very bones had turned to ice. As though, like my son, my hot red blood had turned into something else entirely, something unnatural, something death-dealing.

I blamed myself. I did not have a close relationship with God yet. I was a Christian, and I went to church and learned my Scriptures and sang the hymns I was taught, but it was all superficial then. I didn't yet know the Lord, not really. I thought I must have made a big sin in my life and God was punishing me. I had killed my own son, my Sleiman. And I thought it was the end of the world. There was no future for me. That was it.

And I hated myself.

Fariid didn't blame me. He never whispered a word of blame or guilt. He never looked at me with suspicion. He tried to comfort me. But how could I be comforted when my son was gone? How could I be happy again when my own hands had killed that chubby boy whom I so loved?

They gave him a short funeral at our home, not in the church, because he was still a baby, and that's how these things were done. And they came and took him from me and buried him there, in Damascus. And I hated Damascus after that. I still hate it, to this day.

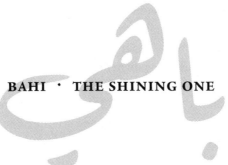

BAHI · THE SHINING ONE

Damascus, 1957

In those days, the flavor of religious diversity that had always been part of our culture somehow changed. Until the *nakba* in Palestine, Arabs lived peaceably and harmoniously with their neighbors of any religion. Everyone knew the faith and tradition of the families around them, which families were Muslim, which Christian, which Jewish, but such differences were honored and respected, not sources of tension or distrust.

But that changed in the latter half of the twentieth century. Between the religious divisions that were created by the insertion of a Jewish state and the backlash of predominantly Muslim countries against Western Christian powers, differences of faith among neighbors began to feel like a threat.

But we hadn't recognized that yet.

After Sleiman — my first Sleiman — died, I was crying all the time. All the time I cried, because I missed my baby, and I blamed myself for what had happened to him. And everywhere I looked, I saw the lack of him. The baby cot was empty, and the stroller was empty, and the chair at the table was empty. Everything was empty and cold. And I cried all the time. And I prayed for a baby to fill the empty places.

My third baby, a girl, was born less than a year after Sleiman's death. We named her Lena. And I loved her. I was so glad she had come.

But she was not like her brother, who had been happy and smiling always. Lena cried and complained from the moment she was born. She cried so much I thought there must be something wrong with her. But the older women in my family and my neighborhood told me it was because I was crying all the time when I carried Lena inside of me. Maybe they were right. Maybe these are how things go. I don't know. All I know is that Lena complained and cried all throughout her early childhood. But she was a beautiful baby, and she helped to fill the emptiness around me and within me. And I loved her.

After that, life became easy for us. After I lost my baby, God turned his face back to me, and he was gracious unto me. I delivered two more children: another boy whom we named again after his grandfather, Sleiman, and a girl, Salaam. I named her Salaam because at that time, there seemed always to be tensions and wars and rumors of wars, and all I wanted, all I longed for, was peace. I wanted to live in peace.

"Sleiman" means peace, too, of course, though he was named after his grandfather and his older brother — both of whom were dead by the time of Moni's birth. That's what we called him, my second Sleiman, "Moni," because his sister Lena, who was only eighteen months older than him, couldn't say "Sleiman" and named him that instead. And because "Moni" helped to distinguish him from his brother, whom I kept always in my heart.

And the children grew and flourished, and our family was happy again.

Damascus had beautiful parks. The other families in our neighborhood had servants who lived with the family and who would take care of the children while their mothers visited one another and gossiped over tea. The servants would take the children to the park and let them play, or walk with the babies around the paths. We had a servant who would come in and help with the housework, cleaning and preparing the meals. But I did not let her watch my children. They were too precious to me. I alone had the care of them.

Neither would I let May help much with her younger siblings. I remembered my own childhood, being one of the eldest, with my sister Rose, how we had to help my mother all the time and how much I didn't like it. I would have preferred to read and attend to my lessons. And I wanted May to have the opportunities I didn't have — I wanted to give all my children those opportunities.

And they were all clever; all of them were good students. When they went to school, I would help them with their homework. They would sit around the table, each with their own work, and I would do my knitting, and they would ask me when they needed help. Because I was a teacher, I knew what sorts of questions their teachers would ask, and I wanted my children to be prepared and to get good grades. And they did.

Fariid was very proud of them. He would come home from work in the evenings, and he would be tired and grumpy. And the children would run to him and tell him of their schoolwork and the good grades they had received, and his whole face would brighten.

But only God is changeless, not our lives. And when my youngest child, Salaam, was still in diapers, the solid ground on which we stood seemed to start shifting beneath us. Abdel Nasser came to power in Egypt then, and he made no secret of his dream of a pan-Arab republic. To achieve it, he began with Syria, wooing the Syrian government to join in the movement.

And Fariid began to worry. These so-called pan-Arab sentiments expressed by Abdel Nasser and his ilk seemed, to my husband, to be decidedly Islamic in flavor. We had begun to notice that our once-easy relationships with friends and neighbors, colleagues and servants who were Muslim were no longer quite as uncomplicated. Fariid was afraid, with the push toward pan-Arabism in Syria, a mostly Muslim country, that we, as Christians, wouldn't be safe. He wanted to move. Again.

Four of Fariid's brothers had stayed in Beirut after the *nakba* and built lives for themselves there. They had married and were raising families of their own. And Labiibeh, "Teta *Im* Fariid" as she was known by then, had moved to be with her sons after the death of her husband. So Fariid wanted to move there, back to Beirut, where his family was — where my sister Rose still lived with her husband — and where we would be surrounded by many more Arab Christians like us.

When he told me of his plans, I started to cry. I have never taken well to change. I'm scared of it. I did not trust in God's providence, and so much of my adult life had been spent wandering, fleeing from fear in one place to another that was filled with uncertainty. I did not want to go. But Fariid was insistent.

Of course, the reason we had left Beirut in the first place — the lack of work permits for Palestinians — was still an obstacle to rebuilding our life there. We couldn't, at first, get Lebanese identities. But somehow, Fariid's brother George who was living in Lebanon managed to get fake ID cards for us. God knows how he did it. And through friends and neighbors and contacts, he sent these illegal IDs to us. But they weren't right. There were little mistakes peppered throughout all of them. None of the birth dates on them was correct — not for Fariid or the children. Only mine had the right date. And I was so scared that the Lebanese authorities would see the inconsistencies and arrest us at the border or take Fariid from us, and the children and I would starve.

But Fariid had made up his mind. So as soon as the IDs arrived, he resigned his job in Damascus, and we packed up our belongings — as much as we could take with us — and we took our children and moved to Beirut to start over. To begin again.

This time, though, we could afford to start from less humble beginnings. Right away, we rented an apartment across the street from the American University of Beirut, AUB. The neighborhood we lived in was exclusively for rich people, although we were not rich. But being educated is being rich; this is how it was there. Our apartment was on the third floor of the building, and it was nice — no leaky ceiling, good quality, spacious enough for our family. Across the alley on the side was a very good bakery where we would get fresh bread every morning, so close we could send one of the children to fetch our order.

Our apartment building was located in West Beirut, which was a Muslim quarter, but the building was owned by a Christian man, an Armenian. And the Armenians don't like Muslims, because the Armenians have historically been persecuted by Muslims. So the landlord refused to rent his apartments to Muslims, and everyone in our building were Christians. But our neighbors in the other buildings — our Muslim neighbors — were not fanatics or fundamentalists. They were well educated and well-to-do families, like ours. So we got along with everyone around us. We would stay in that apartment for more than a decade, and I would grow to love it as my home.

But at first, I did not love the apartment, or Beirut. I found the people there to be snobby and superficial. The women I met spent their lives showing off their wealth and gossiping nonsense and nothings to one another. I did not participate in these things. I just wanted to raise my children and read my books. But I felt they looked down on me for that reason. And in those first months, I was miserable.

I had my sister Rose, though. She lived in a house they had built in the mountains outside of Beirut, not too far from us. You could catch a glimpse of the Mediterranean from the front porch of her home. They had moved there soon after their last child, Kamil, was born. When he was delivered, the doctor took one look at his sweet, large, round face — too round — and told Rose, "This son you have delivered is going to be a *majnoon*, a crazy one." Rose didn't know what the doctor meant. Distraught, she sought the advice of one of our cousins on my mother's side, Dr. Raja 'Asfour, who reassured her a little. "No, he's not *majnoon*, but he is not normal, and he will never be." They didn't call it Down syndrome then.

So Rose and her husband Hanna built their house in the fresh air of the mountains and hoped that their son's health would improve. And I would take my children there to visit with her and to enjoy the fresh fruits and vegetables that grew plentifully in the gardens and orchards of that place.

Rose asked Hanna to help Fariid get a job at the company where Hanna worked, Bank of America, and he did. So Fariid began as an office manager in one of the branches of the bank there in Beirut, and he liked his job and worked hard at it and once again was promoted quickly.

We sent our girls, May, Lena, and eventually Salaam to an English school near our home. Our son Moni went to an American evangelical school; it was nearby, too, but it was a coeducational school — the first time we experienced such a thing! — and we did not feel it was a good place for our daughters.

A year or two after we moved to Beirut, my parents brought my youngest siblings there, too. They lived nearby to us, so I saw them often. And I socialized with my husband's brothers and their wives. And all of the families, our families, Fariid's and mine, lived within a walkable distance from each other.

We all belonged to the local parish, All Saints' Church. And I went back to singing in the choir — along with Rose and Hanna, like it used to be when we were young. Every Sunday we would all go to church. All Saints' used to belong to the English community, and they gave it to the Palestinians in Lebanon. It was the only Anglican Church, and it was English-speaking, but there were so many Anglican families that came from Palestine, that they gave it to us, and it became an Arabic-speaking church. We had our priest, always Palestinian, and it was overlooking the Mediterranean — a very pretty view — with a big terrace in front of the church. And I had grown in faith by then, but I was not yet as mature as I would become later. It was only when I came to the States that I was able to take Bible classes and learn about the stories there and my own faith and be fully opened to the truth.

But in Beirut, I went to that church with my husband and children, my siblings and in-laws. And everybody knew everybody else from Palestine. The children went to Sunday school, and May, my eldest daughter, helped to lead it, and she was old enough to be involved in the youth group by then, too. After church, we would all go to my mother-in-law's house, Teta *Im* Fariid's, for coffee, and she made cookies or cake.

Teta *Im* Fariid lived very close by to us. After her husband's death, she had moved to Beirut and lived with my brother-in-law George. And I liked her very much. And she liked me. She used to tell the wives of my husband's brothers, "Go learn from Fariid's wife"; that's what she always called me — either Fariid's wife or *Im* Sleiman, Sleiman's mother. And she would tell my sisters-in-law, "Go learn from *Im* Sleiman how to raise your children and teach them." Teta *Im* Fariid had a servant, a woman named Samiye, who lived with her who would help her clean and take care of the house. Everyone there, especially in that neighborhood, had servants to help with the housework and cook and clean, but I did not, because we were not as wealthy. But Teta *Im* Fariid would send her servant to my house once a week to help me with the housework. And I was very grateful for that. And so I began to grow accustomed to my life again and to enjoy it.

THE DRESSES
A STORY

In those days, there was a brief period of respite in the Middle East. It was before the 1967 war in Israel, well before the *intifadas* had begun. And next door in Lebanon, too, interreligious tensions were perhaps on the rise, but still below the surface, still unseen by those whose wealth or education insulated them.

When civil war finally erupted in Lebanon, Palestinian Christians would find themselves caught between the proverbial rock and hard place. As Palestinians, they were viewed by the native Lebanese Christians as part of the problems created decades earlier by the influx of mostly Muslim refugees from Palestine, violently evicted from their homes by the brutal tactics of a nascent Israel. But as Christians, they were seen by their Palestinian compatriots eking out a living in Lebanon as allies of a Christian-dominated bureaucratic system that shut out the poorer, often less well-educated Muslims. Palestinian Christians would be viewed with suspicion — at best — from both sides.

But in the late 50s and early 60s, Bahi and her family were still unaware of the growing tension. They had settled into life in Beirut, and Bahi imagined that, finally, she could put down roots that would not be torn up again. She visited with her extended family, raised her children, and tended to her hardworking husband. She could finally relax.

Her eldest child, May, was a particular source of pride and the focus of much of Bahi's attention. May was a very good student, well liked among her peers and admired as an exemplar by the older generation. Now twelve years old, May was on the cusp of leaving her girlhood. Bahi marveled to watch how May moved between the two worlds — one minute playing with dolls in all her innocence and the next begging her mother to pull out the iron to straighten and tame her dark curls.

May's closest friend was actually her aunt, Elham. Bahi's youngest sister was born nine days after May. Of course, Bahi had been separated from her parents and siblings by then. Elham was born in Cairo after Bahi had given birth to May in that dingy apartment in Beirut mere months after the *nakba*. But Bahi had known back in February of 1948, before they all had to flee, that her mother was pregnant with her last baby just as Bahi had conceived her first.

How she had grumbled when her mother had shared the news. She hadn't said anything too pointed out loud, of course. She didn't dare — certainly not in her father's hearing. But she had complained to Fariid at the time. "How can she still be bearing children? It's not her turn. It's unseemly."

All these years later, the thought of her and her mother's simultaneous pregnancies still made her shake her head. But in the end, she gave thanks to God for her baby sister who had grown to become such an agreeable companion for Bahi's own daughter. From their early days in Damascus until now, Elham and May had always played together and talked together. And they would have each other during this often-difficult transition between childhood and youth. Bahi was glad of that.

She could hear them now in one of the back bedrooms, laughing and giggling with each other. It was a Saturday. Bahi was in the kitchen, preparing the noonday meal they would share together, and she smiled to hear the girls' joyful voices. Fariid had taken the younger ones to the park for the morning; he was careful that way — always wanting to spend time with his children even when he worked so hard, always helping Bahi with the housework in little ways, unlike all the other husbands and fathers they knew. Bahi reflected on these things and whispered out loud a quick thanksgiving to God as she mashed the garlic in the bowl before her into a paste.

Samiye walked into the kitchen at the tail end of Bahi's prayer. She murmured a soft "amen," like a confirmation of Bahi's gratitude, though the housemaid must not have heard the petition that preceded the traditional conclusion. But Samiye was like that: a small but not insignificant support to Bahi's life.

Samiye didn't actually work for Fariid and Bahi. She was Teta *Im* Fariid, Bahi's mother-in-law's servant, an older woman whose work in others' homes helped provide for her extended family. But Teta *Im* Fariid knew how hard Bahi worked to care for her family, too. The mother-in-law approved of and appreciated Bahi's industriousness. So she sent Samiye to Fariid and Bahi's home once a week, to help Bahi with the housework and the endless chores.

Samiye was currently doing some light cleaning in all the rooms of the house and had come into the kitchen briefly to replenish her supplies — and, coincidentally, to affirm Bahi's prayer of thanksgiving. The two women glanced at each other and smiled in the midst of their tasks. They understood each other; though they didn't share a religion, they found commonality in their mutual faith, nonetheless. Samiye was Muslim but Palestinian, like Bahi, and they both knew that the one God heard their prayers, regardless of whether they were whispered in the name of Jesus.

Still wrapped in her own thoughts, Bahi jumped when she heard Samiye's scream a few minutes later. "*Yamma*," she exclaimed, warding away bad news. Bahi quickly rinsed her hands, drying them on her apron as she ran to May's bedroom at the back of the apartment, where the scream had come from.

When she burst into the room, she was confronted by a scene that took her a minute to understand. May and Elham apparently been playing dress-up. They had found, likely tucked back in a closet somewhere, Bahi's own engagement and wedding dresses. Bahi couldn't help but smile fondly when she saw the girls engulfed in the fabric still too big for them. But the dresses themselves elicited mixed feelings from Bahi. On the one hand, they were the reminders of her marriage to Fariid, which she had been giving God thanks for only a few minutes earlier. But they also brought to mind the terrible trauma of those last months in Palestine.

The dresses had not been easy to come by. The engagement dress had been purchased early enough in 1947 that it was a premade item. And it was good quality. But it had been extremely expensive, with so many shops and merchants unable to get the materials they needed during that time. The dress was a light blue with a layer of taffeta beneath the chiffon overlay, with taffeta ribbons of the same blue woven in wide, horizontal stripes through the skirt and short puffed sleeves jutting out from a high-necked but form-fitting top.

By the time Aniiseh and Bahi were ready to shop for Bahi's wedding dress, though, they were unable to buy it premade since only Jewish merchants owned the shops that sold such money-making garments by then; all the other Arab merchants, if not killed, had been threatened with violence and had lost their trade. So Bahi and Aniiseh had managed to purchase only the fabric necessary and had engaged a seamstress to quickly sew the finished garment. The woman had to spend a number of nights at the family's home until the dress was completed, since it was unsafe for her to return to her own house and come back every day. Everything had seemed rushed then; everything done under duress. And Bahi had been afraid that her wedding dress would be of poor quality as a result. But it wasn't. It was beautiful, with long lace sleeves and a full-length skirt in perfect ivory.

When Bahi and Fariid had fled Haifa that terrible spring, carrying only the basic necessities, some cash, and Bahi's jewelry, they had left her engagement and wedding dresses behind. She had hated to do it, but she could fit only so much in the small suitcase they took with them, and she knew that such garments, as much sentimental value as they had to her, would be useless to them as refugees in Beirut. And besides, when they left, they had still assumed they would be back one day, within a few weeks, months, at least within the year. Bahi imagined she would come back to her newly-wed apartment in Haifa to resume her life there and have access to these things that she cherished.

But when it became clear that they had been exiled from their country and denied the right to return, Bahi was distraught about all the things she had left behind, her wedding and engagement dresses among them. Luckily, Fariid's family, thanks to his father's position in the Anglican mission in Haifa, enjoyed some amount of immunity from the horror that Israel inflicted on so many other families who stayed behind. The Owaydas had gone to Fariid and Bahi's apartment weeks after the couple's departure and salvaged many of their possessions. Little by little, through friends and acquaintances, through Fariid's brothers who eventually sought refuge in Beirut then, too, through the legitimate UN troops and the illegal agents who crossed borders, Bahi reacquired some of her most treasured belongings, including her dresses that now hung from May and Elham's not-quite-teenage bodies.

May was dressed in the long white gown. The hem dragged along the floor, and May was tripping over the ends. Elham, her dark curls bouncing as she laughed out loud, looked small in the sea of blue that engulfed her. They were enjoying themselves greatly. But Samiye, the servant woman, was horrified. She accosted her mistress as soon as Bahi entered the room. "*Ya haram!*" she exclaimed. "How will you let these children play with such beautiful, rich dresses?" The girls paused in their play and glanced up anxiously at Bahi, wondering whether they were about to be in trouble. But Bahi just shrugged. "Why should I stop them? They are having fun. Just look at them."

"*Ye ye ye ye ye!*" Samiye replied. "My daughter is engaged to a man whom she will marry soon, and we have nothing so beautiful to give her. What a waste." Shaking her head at Bahi's foolishness, the woman left the room to continue her work in the house.

Later that afternoon, the noonday meal finished and the kitchen clean again, Bahi went into May's room. The girls were gone, and the two dresses were left sprawling on one of the beds. Bahi picked them up and hung them carefully on hangers. She gathered an old sheet and wrapped it around the two dresses, placing the whole bundle back on the mattress. She found Samiye near the front door gathering her things as she readied herself to leave. "Wait, Samiye," Bahi said softly to her. "Before you go, come with me. There's something I have for you."

Bahi brought Samiye to her daughters' bedroom and laid the soft package with the dresses bound up together in the woman's outstretched arms. "Take these," she said, "and give them to your daughter. May she be radiant on her wedding day and as happy in her marriage as I have been in mine." Samiye stood there for a moment, speechless, cradling the bundle in her arms like an overgrown baby. Finally, she looked at Bahi with tears in her eyes. "*Yslim 'uyuunik*," she said. "May your eyes be blessed." And she left.

That evening, May asked her mother what happened to the dresses she and Elham had been playing with that morning, and Bahi told her. "But weren't you sad to give them away?" May asked. "Didn't you want to keep them?"

"*Habiibti*, what did I want them for?" Bahi responded, smiling at her daughter. "I have my marriage; I have my family. The dresses are just things, and Samiye has much better use for them."

BAHI · THE SHINING ONE

Beirut, 1974

In those days, in Lebanon, especially in Beirut, as tensions between Muslims and Christians, Palestinians and Lebanese grew, so did the tensions between one generation and the next. I suppose Beirut was no different from other places throughout the world at the time, in the 1960s and early 1970s, before its civil war began. I just remember feeling torn, more and more, between the way I had been raised, the way I had always expected to raise my children, and the desires and demands that May, Lena, Moni, and Salaam all had as they grew. And I began to feel torn, too, between two cultures, between Arab ways and American ones.

By the mid-1960s, May had started college at the American University of Beirut. I had worked so hard, focused so much of my energy on May; she was my eldest, and I was anxious that she should go to the university. I was anxious for all my children to go and be well educated. Even if I had to tear off my flesh to get a university education for my children, I would have done it. I was insistent about it. And because May was my first child, she was the first to go. And she got into the American University of Beirut, and I was so happy and proud.

And when she went there, all of a sudden, everything seemed to be from or about the States. May went to an American college;

her professors were all American; the way she lived her life became American, too. She went out with groups of young people on her own, boys and girls. She dressed in maxi dresses and miniskirts. She straightened her hair and confided in me her dreams of independence — and of maybe meeting an American man, tall and free-thinking and different from the Arab boys she knew.

And part of me was so glad! I had always held on to this hidden, secret longing for the States and for the way of life it represented — ever since I was educated by the likes of Ms. Jones and Ms. Guile in all their strict but free-spirited wisdom. I was happy that May was laying claim to that kind of opportunity; I hoped that my younger children would, too.

I still wished that we had accepted Mr. Foley's offer all those years ago and gone to the States when we had the opportunity. Because if we had, we would have assimilated into that culture, and I could have raised my children there, and we would not have worried so much about what people said about our children, about us. But we *did* worry about these things. Fariid worried about them more than me, but if I'm honest, I did, too. I was hurt by the things people said.

Every week it seemed, one or other of my sisters-in-law, the gossipy ones, would tsk-tsk at me, shaking their heads: "*Ye ye ye!* We saw May walking alongside a boy on Hamra Street yesterday!" they'd say. Or "*Ye! Ya ayba shoum!* What a shame! I saw May with the youth group from church and her skirt was so short! How could you let her leave the house like that?" I didn't dare tell them that *I* had made May's skirt — like all of her clothes — myself, to her specific requests. We would debate together over the length; May wanted the hem as short as the skirts of the other girls in her set, but we both knew that length would be too scandalous for Fariid to accept, so together we compromised. But *was* it too short? And was May leaving herself open to the scathing gossip of my own generation when she went about as she did with her friends from the university?

But even as a child, May had been a trustworthy daughter. And now, she did nothing behind our backs; she was never secretive or sly. She always confided in me, told me where she would be, whom she was with; I met all of her friends, boys and girls, and many of her American professors. She brought them home to share in the noonday meal, and we got to know them all.

So in time, I grew used to the idea that May was becoming an American, and I tried to help Fariid grow accustomed to it, too. And little by little, he did. He stopped worrying about what people might say about her and took more and more pride in her many achievements.

She graduated from AUB with high honors. She won so many prizes, and all of us, her father and I, and all her siblings, were so proud of her.

After her graduation, she was hired by her professors to work in their offices, doing research and administration for them, or tutoring the younger students. And she enrolled in graduate school at the university, too. She became a well-educated, well-respected, well-traveled young woman.

As part of her work with the professors, she took trips to London and Athens and Paris. I remember the first time she took one of these trips. She worked for a summer tutoring the son of one of her professors in Greece. And the whole time she was gone, I had this feeling of unrest in my heart and in my throat. I wrote her a letter every day until she came home. I had never been separated from her like that. And I was more naive than she was, because I had never traveled myself, not really. Of course, we had been to Cairo for our honeymoon, and we had fled one city and another in our lives together, Fariid and I, but I had never really been to different places, to Europe and to the West.

Let me tell you about the first time I went to Europe, after May had graduated from AUB — her first graduation. Fariid was given the opportunity to go to London and Paris for a special training with his company, Bank of America, for a promotion. And they told him that he could bring his wife for the last week of the training in London and the couple of days that would follow in Paris.

At first, I didn't want to go; it would be the first time in my life that I left my children. But Fariid wanted me to come, since so many of his colleagues in this training were bringing their wives during those ten days, and Fariid thought it would make him look bad if I didn't go. And eventually, May talked me into it, too; she wanted me to have the new experience.

So I decided to go, and I took an airplane from Beirut to London. It was only the second time that I was on an airplane, and I was feeling happy and excited by the time I boarded my flight. Fariid met me at the airport and took me to the hotel — a very nice hotel. I was surprised to see the room had a king-size bed. All our married life, Fariid and I had slept separately in the same room but in different beds — a small single bed for each of us. And now, we would sleep together for the first time in this great big king bed!

I spent a wonderful week in London. May had given me the name of a friend she had met in her travels who lived there, and this girl met me and took me around. I was a tourist, and I saw so many of the sights there. And I shopped a lot and bought gifts for my children, and in the evenings, Fariid and I would go to the theaters and have dinners together.

And then we flew to Paris. Our stay there was just a few days, and it was the first time in my life that I said no to my husband. In Paris, Fariid's training took place only in the mornings, and then he had the afternoon off. All he wanted to do was go back to the hotel room after lunch and watch TV, but I refused. I insisted that we go together to see the sights of Paris. I had been studying French in a little language school not far from our house in Beirut for four years. May had helped me to find the school and enroll in the classes there. And I learned the language, even though my other children and my husband laughed at me because I was a grown woman going to school. But I always wanted to learn; I was always hungry for more knowledge. So I insisted that Fariid and I go out into the streets of Paris and see things, and I spoke in French and took us around the city, all the while Fariid mumbling that I was just showing off!

But we had a good time on that trip, and I was happy when I went home to my children.

It was not long after we returned from that trip that May brought Joe to the house for the first time. For a long while, she had been dating another American man, and she liked him, but then they stopped going out together when he left the country for a job. And I worried about her. She wasn't old by today's standards, but then, things were different. I worried that she would not find someone and settle down and be happy. Always, in my heart, I prayed, "Please, God, send someone to May who will make her happy." When I confided my fears to my own mother, Mama intervened, and May wore the cross that my mother gave her. And a few months later, she met Joe at a party.

They were introduced to each other by Peter Jennings, who was a journalist in Beirut then, too, and not as famous yet as he would later become. But May was friends with all these Americans, most of whom had come to Beirut to report on the civil war that was building and finally broke out in Lebanon in 1975. So May was at a party at Peter Jennings's home in Beirut, and he introduced her to Joe.

And because she was never secretive, whenever May met a boy she liked, she would bring him to our house. We wouldn't tell the rest of the family; they would gossip about her. I wouldn't even let her tell Elham these things. But I wanted her to bring her friends home so that we could meet them and get to know them. And she did.

So we met Joe very early on; almost as soon as May met him, she brought him to our house. And I made *heshwey* and *sfeeha* and *wara 'anab*. And I liked Joe immediately. In my heart, I knew he was the answer to my prayers for May. But I didn't say anything then.

Their romance is not my story to tell; I cannot say how it happened. It took a year or two, if I remember correctly. And then one day, May told us that Joe was coming to see us. "He wants to marry me," she said. "But he is insisting that he follow our customs and our culture. He wants to come and ask for my hand in marriage from you."

So we knew that Joe was coming to ask for May's hand, and we were so excited and happy about it.

On the day he came, he had dressed formally, in a suit and tie, his hair combed back. He was a very tall man; at over six feet, he towered over May by more than a foot. But we could tell that he was trying to make himself smaller, not quite so imposing, perfectly polite. I think he was nervous, too, though he must have known what our answer would be.

He knocked at the door. Salaam, who was a young teenager by then, had been told strictly to keep out of the day's events, to go to her room and stay there when Joe came over. But she was always mischievous, and when Joe knocked on the door, Salaam beat us all to it. Before we had made it to the hallway, we heard the patter of her feet and the click of the door handle. She swung the door open, saw Joe standing there in his suit and tie, and yelled at the top of her voice: "*Inteh majnoon!*" "You're crazy!" She ran away again, leaving the door open and Joe stunned but bemused. Months later, on a trip to London for work, he brought back a shirt for Salaam that he had had made in England that said "MAJNOON" in big black letters on the back.

But that day, after Joe's initial shock, we invited him into the living room, and we all sat down together. Joe turned to Fariid and said to him, "Mr. Owayda, I would like to ask for your daughter's hand in marriage."

And Fariid replied, "Yes, of course. It is an honor to us to have you as our son-in-law."

And I had tears in my eyes. Because this is what May deserved, what my eldest child, who had held my heart for so long, who had achieved so much, who had worked so hard, deserved — someone to love her and make her happy. And I couldn't wait to begin planning her wedding.

THE WEDDING

A STORY

In those days, things had started. It started when Christian militants attacked a bus full of Muslims going to Beirut. It started because the Muslims had grown hatred for the Christians in their hearts, and the Christians hated the Muslims, too. It started because the bus attack was just the straw that broke the camel's back; it was an excuse for Muslims and Christians to show their hatred for each other and start killing each other.

The Palestinian refugees had a lot to do with it. The Palestinians wanted to have the same rights as the Lebanese who had always lived there, and they were willing to do anything to get what they wanted. And the Lebanese government was weak and dysfunctional; it quickly collapsed against such pressures. There was no one in control — no one to keep the violent people, the *majaniin*, "the morons," as Bahi called them, in check.

Everything began closing down. Shops and stores and businesses. Every day, it got worse. Militants, "morons with guns," would set up checkpoints and pull people from their cars to interrogate them and beat them if they didn't like something about them, if they thought you were on the wrong side. People would be killed randomly, it seemed, for no reason, and their bodies thrown under bridges. People would just disappear, and their friends and family never knew what happened to them. Young men and women, people going to work or school, going about their daily lives. No one was safe.

And that was when May married Joe. Like her mother before her, May's wedding took place in the midst of violence and uncertainty, chaos and killing. Of course, marrying an American came with certain advantages that the young Bahi and Fariid, Palestinians, would never have known. Despite the clothing stores and ready-made shops being closed, May and Joe took a trip to London to purchase all the needed items for their wedding. They met May's sister Lena and her boyfriend Awni there (the couple were studying for their graduate degrees at separate schools in Scotland), and the four of them enjoyed the sights, security, and shopping of the city together. May's wedding dress and outfits for her younger sister Salaam and their mother Bahi were all bought from the luxury shops of London. And it was good for Lena to share that experience with her sister, since the civil war made it too dangerous for Lena to return to Beirut for the actual wedding.

And Joe's American citizenship, American press pass, and American dollars offered extra protection, too. Both sides of the civil conflict were eager to lure the power and wealth of the United States to their own ends and didn't dare risk interfering with a reporter from the West. Joe generously showed his gratitude for their protection of him, his bride, and her family, handing out dollars to the reaching hands that met him at every apartment building or hotel door.

And so May and Joe prepared for the big day. Their invitations were made and delivered — mostly by hand, since the postal service was unreliable on a good day — to friends and family, announcing the wedding ceremony in the chapel of AUB; May's own childhood church was in a different part of the city and too dangerous to get to. But only a few days before the wedding, the AUB chapel was shelled and rendered unusable. So the couple pivoted and were married by the Rev. Samir Kafity (who would go on to serve as the twelfth bishop of the Episcopal Diocese of Jerusalem) on April 17, 1976 in the concrete chapel of the nearby Near East School of Theology instead. Even so, the whole wedding party had to steal themselves to the church, keeping an eye out for snipers hidden in the windows above them and praying for a pause in the relentless small-rocket attacks.

The members of May's family in attendance were much smaller in number than they would have been otherwise. Most of the families of her many aunts (on her mother's side) and uncles (on her father's side) had fled the worsening conflict and had sought what they thought was temporary refuge in other countries — Egypt, Jordan, the United Kingdom, and the United States. Save Salaam, even May's siblings were absent.

But the wedding was a joyous occasion, nonetheless. The priest in his white cassock and stole, the beautiful bride, light brown skin glowing in contrast to the white lace gown, the groom, tall and slender and beaming with pride. The organist played the wedding march; the priest pronounced the rites in a mixture of English and Arabic, and the sounds of war and violence stilled, miraculously, for a few blessed moments. As the service ended, May's grandmother, Teta Aniiseh, sang out the traditional Arabic blessings, and the women present chorused with celebratory lulus.

Fariid and Bahi were delighted to welcome Joe, in all his gentleness and Americanness, into the family. He obviously worshiped their daughter and had already proven to be caring and concerned for May — and all her kith and kin. And as a journalist, Joe had plenty of photographer friends who could capture the ceremony and reception so that the joyful day — even in the midst of the chaos surrounding it — could be remembered and shared with those unable to be present.

It was dangerous to be out in the dusk or dark, so the wedding was held in the morning with a champagne reception following at one of the nearby hotels — a hotel that hosted many foreign journalists among its longer-term residents and was therefore relatively safe from attacks by combatants. Still, Joe had paid a number of the armed "morons" to stand guard at the hotel doors and along the close streets so that wedding guests could make it to the party without being harmed.

But morons will be morons, and the party didn't end without incident.

As the reception began winding down — early, as the anxious guests were eager to get to the relative safety of their own homes —

one of the guards brought in a large present wrapped in colorful paper. He handed it to May, who broke away from conversation with confusion to take the gift from the stranger. She unwrapped it in front of her remaining guests to reveal a shiny Kalashnikov. There was even a white bow tied around the barrel. The hotel hall grew suddenly silent until the guard gave an awkward laugh. "It's a joke!" he said, in self-defense.

May offered him a scathing look in thanks and handed the gun to her father, who quickly and quietly took it away. The bridal couple returned to their guests, but the party had clearly ended for good; the magical spell of love and joy protecting the wedding-goers — for just a few hours — from the terror of the past year of war had been broken.

BAHI · THE SHINING ONE

Beirut, 1975

In those days, the armed elements on both sides took over, and the civil war broke out in full force. We had fled Haifa because the Zionists were killing people and destroying their homes and violating us everywhere, and we lived in fear, so we fled. And when we had made a life for ourselves in Damascus, the threat of violence and hatred that surrounded us when Abdel Nassar came to power in Egypt seemed too great, and so we fled. And now, here we were again.

We had such a nice life in Beirut. We had so many good opportunities and we lived among our family and friends — all of us different but all of us happy. And then these armed morons come with their hatred, and it started all over, from the beginning, the same pattern of terror and fear. I prayed for our survival. I prayed that we would all make it to see the next morning.

One day there would be bread, and the next day there would be no bread, because the armed militants had confiscated all the flour going to the bakery. One day there would be fruit, and the next day none. One day there would be meat, and the following day, there was no meat to be found anywhere.

The Palestinian Muslims fought Lebanese Christians. And the Lebanese Muslims, who were poor and not as well educated as their

Christian countrymen, allied themselves with the Palestinians, hoping to overturn a largely Christian government and topple the elite system.

And it became very dangerous, especially dangerous for us, for my family. I was scared whenever Fariid would go to work even. Because, to the Muslims, he was Christian, and to the Lebanese, he was Palestinian. And all those people with hatred in their hearts would find a reason to hate him, because we were Palestinian Christians.

Even in AUB, the tensions began flaring up. Lena, thanks be to God, had graduated just as the worst violence began to erupt. Along with her serious boyfriend, a Jordanian named Awni, she had left for Scotland to take up graduate studies there. On the day she was due to travel, Fariid asked Joe, our soon-to-be son-in-law, to take Lena to the airport, and Joe instantly agreed.

For many months, Joe had paid a chauffeur to drive him for longer journeys or on days when the danger seemed more pronounced. This man, the driver, was named Abu Mughrabi, and he was a Muslim who was very loyal to Joe — thanks, in part, to the generosity with which Joe renumerated him for his services. Whenever Joe's chauffeured car encountered one of these makeshift checkpoints that the armed morons had set up in our part of the city, Abu Mughrabi would roll down his window and speak to the militant who had stopped them using the dialect and rhetoric they shared. "Don't concern yourself with my passengers," Abu Mughrabi would say, "They're all American anyway." And the car would be allowed to move on seamlessly.

So when Lena was ready to go to the airport for her flight to Scotland, Joe came in the car with Abu Mughrabi driving. They loaded up her suitcases in the trunk as I kissed my daughter goodbye. I worried about her, of course. She would be so far from home. But I knew other Arab students studied at her university, and Awni would be there, too. She was far safer in Scotland, away from the civil war and the constant fear through which we lived. As Lena got in the car, I reached out to Joe and grabbed his hand. "Thank you," I said, tears in my eyes. "Thank you for getting her there safely. You're an angel."

He smiled and winked at me. "An angel with a moustache!" he replied.

So Lena was safe in Scotland. May spent most of her days with Joe and enjoyed the protections that his American press pass provided. And Salaam was a teenager, a girl still, who lived with us and stayed at home, and I could be relatively certain of her security.

But Moni, my son — my fears for him ate me up. He was in his second year at AUB. At that time, the situation was so bad that the university often closed to protect their students and employees, but the students used the opportunity of days with no lessons to hold rallies to protest the violence erupting all around them. And Moni would participate in these marches, and I was so scared that something would happen to him. Sometimes, these militiamen, the morons, would shoot at the students marching. And some of them were killed. So finally, Fariid put his foot down and demanded Moni stay home. And he did. And besides, very quickly, the protests stopped happening. Even the young people themselves were scared.

Still, we knew Moni would never be safe in such an atmosphere. A young man, a Palestinian Christian. Every day he was at risk, more so than May and Salaam and me, more so even than Fariid.

So during the dark days of that Advent, Fariid spoke to Joe and sought his help. "If Moni stays here," he said, "he will be kidnapped and killed. It would be better if we could send him to finish his education in the States, where he'll be safe. Could you help us find the numbers of some universities there so that we can call and find a place for him somewhere?"

"I can do more than that," Joe said. "My old university, Marquette. They'll accept him; I'm sure of it. I know one of the guys in the admissions office there, in fact. He was in my class at school. Let me put a call in to him and see what they can do."

So Joe called his college and explained the situation, and before Christmas had come, we received word that Moni had been accepted as a student at Marquette. His credits from AUB would transfer easily, and he would start in January.

That Christmas was a somber one in our home. A lavish feast, like I would usually prepare, was not possible; our church was closed; we could not see my parents or Rose and her children, or Fariid's brothers and their families; Lena was absent, and Moni would soon be leaving, too. But we gathered around a small tree Fariid had managed to bring home, and we exchanged a few gifts. Fariid had bought long underwear and a new coat for Moni, and I knitted him a warm sweater, since we knew he was going to need these things in the frigid Milwaukee winter.

Moni's flight was scheduled to depart on a cold morning in early January. As he was packing his one suitcase, I called the bakery next door (thanking God that the phone lines were working at least) and asked the baker to send his boy over with some *manaiish*, Moni's favorite treat. I often made it myself, but even I could admit that the bakery's *manaiish* was as good as it got, the bread perfectly baked, almost crisp on the edges but soft and chewy within, beneath the mixture of thyme and spices and oil that was spread in a thick layer on top.

As I waited for the boy to arrive, I set the kettle to boil. Moni had just emerged from the bedroom, suitcase in hand, when the doorbell rang. "*Ye!* I'm surprised the bakery boy made it over here so fast. I ordered you some *manaiish*; we'll have it with our tea before you go," I told Moni as I walked down the hallway.

But when I opened the door, I was met not by the small baker's boy but by Joe himself.

"Is Moni ready?" he asked hurriedly, forgoing his usual gentlemanly greetings.

"Yes, he's just finished packing. But we were going to eat something before he goes. His flight doesn't leave for a few hours yet."

"I know, but we have to leave now," Joe said. I looked behind him through the bars of the balcony and could see the car in the street below, Abu Mughrabi waiting patiently by the driver's side door. "Right now," Joe repeated to me. "The militias have called a temporary ceasefire. Who knows how long it will last, but it's the safest time for us to go. We won't get another opportunity like this."

By that time, Moni had come up behind me. "Yes, of course," he replied. "Let me just get my suitcase, and we can go." I called for Fariid and Salaam, and the three of us hurriedly said our goodbyes. I kissed Moni's cheeks three times, praying in my heart for his safety, wondering when I would again get the chance to see the sweet face of my son, my second Sleiman, God's gift to me for the one that was taken.

I stood on the balcony waving until I could no longer see the car. And then I turned to retrieve the kettle that had been left screaming on the stove. I poured the water into three cups — not the four I had set out — letting the tears fall silently down my face. I knew I would have to collect myself before I called the rest of my family into the kitchen for the tea. Fariid hated it when I cried. He refused to condone such weakness. But how I longed for my boy. And I had sent him away hungry; he hadn't even gotten to eat his *manaiish*!

When the boy from the bakery finally did show up with Moni's uneaten treats, I set the *manaiish* aside. They were so good, fresh and warm, but I didn't have the heart to eat them now. Sighing, I set about the tasks of my day, nursing my grief quietly in my breast.

It was less than an hour later that the doorbell rang again. I paused in my work and padded slowly to the door to unlock the bolt. When I opened it, there stood Moni, suitcase in hand, sheepish smile on his much beloved face.

"*Smallah alayk! Smallah alayk!*" I exclaimed. "What happened, *habiibi*?"

"We got to the airport, and it was closed. Something about the fighting that had happened overnight. All flights this morning are canceled. They've rescheduled my flight for later this afternoon."

In shock and joy, I hugged him to me. He would have to leave again in a few hours, of course, and risk the journey to the airport all over again, but Joe would take him, and he would be safe, I knew. So in my heart I said, "Thank you, God, thank you, God," for I knew it was God who had done this; it was God's mercy on my mothering heart that brought my boy back to me for just a little more time.

I took Moni by the hand and led him into the apartment toward the kitchen, calling out to his father and sister to come and welcome him back home briefly. And I put the kettle on the stove to heat the water for the tea. And when we four had gathered, I brought out the *manaiish*, still slightly warm, and we ate them together. And I was so happy.

It was a little bit easier to let him go when Joe picked him up for the second time that day. Now at least, I could send him off, well fed, unhurried, assured of our love for him. And he really did leave then.

Of course, I still worried. I knew one of Joe's closest friends, Kevin Waldeck, was going to meet Moni at the US airport, take him to his family home, and for the first night, at least, Moni would have the warmth of companionship and the nourishment of a homemade meal. I prayed to God to bless Kevin. I was so thankful for him. I had sent Moni with two sweaters I had knitted by hand for Kevin's small son and daughter, a gift that I hoped would communicate my gratitude. But after that first night, in that American college so far away from us, how would Moni cope? Would he be happy?

Like everything else in those days, the phone lines were reliably unreliable. The armed morons would dig them up and cut them regularly, for what reason, I don't know. But because of his work, Joe had a line to the States that was always available and working, and he had given Moni that number to call. Two days after Moni left, May and Joe came to our apartment. They had spoken to him on the phone and brought us his updates.

"He arrived safely," Joe said. "And Kevin met him at the airport as promised. He's fine. All is well. You don't need to worry about him anymore."

And I was glad and relieved that Moni had gotten there without any incidents and was being looked after. But that didn't stop me worrying. I found an opportunity to pull May aside, and we spoke quietly together in the kitchen.

"Is he really okay?" I asked her. "Did you talk to him? How is he feeling?"

"I don't know what to tell you, Mama," she responded. "We spoke for twenty minutes or so. I asked him the same thing — how are you feeling? And he said he doesn't feel anything — not happy, not sad, just *there*. He said the snow on the ground is so much that the piles of it off the sidewalks are taller than he is! And it's very, very cold. He told me when he landed and looked out the window and saw all the snow and when he walked through the airport carrying his suitcase and knowing no one, he thought for a moment that he had made a very big mistake. "What have you done to yourself, *ya* Moni?" That's what he told me ran through his head. I think he's just really really homesick, Mama. But you know Moni. He's an optimist at heart. He won't stay down very long, and he'll be making friends in no time."

May was right, and I was hopeful. After all, it surely wasn't a mistake to have sent him. However cold and snowy it was, however lonely he felt, at least he was alive and out of the mess the morons had made of Lebanon. But I ached for all of my children when they struggled through hardship. And I hurt in my heart, because my child was unhappy.

Still, we thought that, with Moni and Lena gone, at least the rest of us would be okay, Fariid and Salaam and I. We thought we wouldn't have to worry quite so much about our family's safety. But we were wrong.

It didn't take long after Moni left to settle into a new routine. Though May was not yet married, she spent most of her days — and even some nights — with Joe, since it was usually too dangerous for her to drive home in the evenings in her yellow VW Beetle. And with Fariid's office and Salaam's school both staying closed more often than not, the three of us grew accustomed to being in each other's company. Sometimes we visited the neighbors in our building or the ones very close by, or they would come visit us, furtively, quietly. And every now and then, when there was a temporary pause in the fighting, Fariid would go out to bring back what supplies he could find.

We knew the owner of the bakery across the alley from us very well. Because of that, we were able to ask him to call us when he had bread available so that we wouldn't leave the house to get some and discover that it was one of those days when there was none to be had. And the baker was a good man, and very nice to us, and he said that he would.

One day, he called to tell us that he had received the ingredients he needed and he had made a lot of bread. "Send your daughter to come and buy as much bread as you need," he said. So we did. Salaam was sixteen or seventeen years old then. As she neared the door to the bakery, one of these morons, these stupid young men, saw her. He knew who she was; he knew she posed no threat to him. But he shot at her anyway. He did it as a joke; he thought it was funny. Who knows whether he meant to kill her. But he shot at her, and the bullet landed right at her feet. She saw it mark the ground in front of her. She ran into the bakery, got our bread, and ran home, just across the alleyway, as fast as she could.

She told us what had happened, and that was the day Fariid first thought about leaving. That incident with Salaam, I think it made us realize that staying in Beirut, waiting the war out and rebuilding our lives, here in the place we had made our home, might not be possible. "I don't think we can stay here much longer," he told me that night. "I am going to ask Joe whether he can help us *all* find a way out." So the next day, we spoke to Joe, and he said he would make some inquiries at the American embassy. We were his soon-to-be wife's family, after all. Perhaps something could be done. And I prayed to God to give me patience, to trust that our lives were in his hand. And we waited for word.

But then, on the night of May's wedding, our patience came to an abrupt end.

The wedding day was beautiful, despite the circumstances. It was the first time in a long while that I had felt so happy. We went to the reception at the hotel afterward, and we were all having a good time. But then, May opened a present, and it was a gun. Fariid took it from her and took it away — I don't know where — but when he came back a few minutes later, he came straight to me. "Find Salaam," he said, "we're leaving."

"Now?" I asked. "But we're enjoying ourselves. We're having fun."

He reached out to hold my elbow and looked into my eyes with an intensity I'd never before seen. "*Khalas, habiibti.* I know it's hard, but we must go. It's a long walk home, and we don't want to be caught in something dangerous."

I found Salaam, and together we said our goodbyes to May and Joe. They would stay at the hotel until their departure to the States in three weeks' time. And Fariid, Salaam, and I went home.

Fariid ushered us through the front door hurriedly and slammed it shut behind us. I could hear him turning the lock firmly. And then there was silence. Until my sobs began. For once, I was unable to hide them.

That evening, there was no electricity. Like everything else in the city, it was unreliable. One day, one minute, we would have light, and the next, everything would be dark. And that night, we were in the dark.

After a light supper, Salaam went to her bedroom and shut the door. Fariid and I considered staying up. My tears had dried, and I wanted to talk about the wedding, to try to relive the brief but brilliant moments of joy. But with dusk closing in on us, it seemed pointless. And besides, we could hear the rat-a-tat-tat of fighting not so distantly; how could we reminisce about the day to such background noise? So we went to bed early.

But neither of us could sleep. The sounds of not-so-distant fighting quickly became a quite-close conflict. The two sides of armed morons had obviously picked tonight to rejuvenate their efforts to slaughter each other, and our neighborhood was caught in the crossfire. We didn't feel safe near the windows — we didn't feel safe anywhere, but especially not near the windows — so we dragged our mattresses into the long hallway of our apartment. We thought we would try to rest there. I knocked on Salaam's door to tell her to come be with us and was surprised to find her fast asleep. The gift of youth, I suppose, to sleep through such things.

I shook her awake and spoke softly to her: "*Yalla,* Salaam, *yalla, habiibti.* Come into the hallway with Baba and me. It's not safe here, exposed to the whole world in your bed by the window."

But she pushed me away. "*Laa' ya,* Mama," she replied sleepily. "It'll be fine. I'm fine. I'm comfy and warm here in bed, and nothing will happen. Let me go back to sleep." She rolled over. In no time, I could hear her breathing regulate into the slow in-and-outs of slumber. I considered waking her again and demanding that she come with me, or enlisting Fariid to do so, but decided against it. Her bedroom window faced the alley at the back, and we were on the third floor. It was unlikely that she would be harmed.

I went back to Fariid and the mattresses in the hallway, and we tried to settle down to sleep ourselves. But it was a vain effort. For an hour or two I tossed and turned. And then the shell hit us.

It must not have hit *us*, of course. It hadn't hit our building, but it had landed right next to it. The sound was terrifying, a loud bang that shook the very walls and that I could feel in my chest even more profoundly than I could hear in my ears. And half the windows of our home — all the windows on the alley side of the building — shattered immediately, blown in by the impact.

Before I had time to even process what had happened, Salaam came flying out her bedroom door, running straight toward me. She collapsed into my arms, and I could feel her body shaking against me violently. She was sobbing, gasping for breath.

"*Shuu?! Shuu malik?!* What's the matter? What's wrong? Are you okay? Are you hurt?!" My questions tumbled out of me as my hands traveled up and down her body, feeling for any obvious injuries, but nothing seemed out of place, no slickness or warmth of blood met my fingertips.

Finally, Salaam calmed down, and the three of us huddled together, clinging to each other, on the mattresses in the hallway until dawn. In the early morning light, with the shells and shooting temporarily quiet, we walked through the rooms of our apartment. Glass was everywhere. Picture frames and mirrors had fallen off the walls and cracked or shattered. And in Salaam's room, her bed was covered with tiny shards of glass from the window and small metal pieces of the shell that must have landed mere feet away.

May managed to find an open line and reached us on the phone later that morning.

"Are you okay?" she asked me. "Joe heard that the fighting was really bad there last night. Is everyone all right?" I began to tell her all we had lived through since we left her reception the day before. But I had gotten through only half the story when Fariid walked into the room. On hearing that May was on the phone, he took it from me and asked her to call Joe to the line. Ever the stoic, Fariid waited patiently, but I had been married to him for nearly thirty years, and I saw the set of his jaw, the slight tremor in his hand, the anxiety behind the irises of his eyes. He was scared. My husband was very, very scared.

I could hear Joe's deep hello through the phone on Fariid's ear. Fariid told him what had happened, how close the shell must have landed, how narrow Salaam's escape had been this time.

"We can't wait any longer," Fariid said. "We need to get out. Now."

I couldn't hear Joe's response, but only a few minutes later, Fariid thanked him and said goodbye. In the afternoon, the newlyweds came to see us.

"I spoke to my contacts at the embassy and explained the situation," Joe told us. "It's helpful, I think, that we're finally married. Since May is now my wife...." He said the word hesitatingly, lovingly, like he still couldn't believe it was a word that described my daughter to him. "Since May is now my wife, all of you are my family. It means we could speed up the process. You have an appointment at the embassy tomorrow." He pulled a piece of paper out of his breast pocket and handed it to Fariid. I caught a glimpse of his writing on it — block-like numbers and letters that told us when to go and the name of the person to speak to.

The fighting on the night of May's wedding must have depleted all the combatants' resources, because a temporary ceasefire held for the next few days, and we were able to accomplish efficiently all the tasks assigned to us by the agent at the US embassy. At our first meeting with him, we were given special forms to take to the physicians at the hospital at AUB. We were given priority over all the other patients to see the doctors there for our physicals — Fariid, Salaam, and I — and they instructed us to return the completed forms to the embassy as soon as possible. Fariid took them there himself the same afternoon.

Before the week was over, our paperwork was all turned in, our photographs had been taken, and Joe had received assurances from his contacts that our applications would be quickly processed and approved. We would be able to leave Beirut before the summer heat set in.

May and Joe left first, only three weeks after their wedding. Joe was bringing her to meet his family in the suburbs of Chicago, and then they planned to settle down in the city and start their life there. They stopped by our apartment on their way to the airport, in the car driven by the ever-faithful Abu Mughrabi.

It wasn't as hard to say goodbye to May as it had been with my other children. She had Joe by her side, and I knew she was blissfully happy. Plus, we would be close on her heels. In a few more weeks, the first step of our immigration process would be complete, and we'd have the visas we needed to make the trip to the States ourselves. And the agents at the embassy had assured us that by the time we arrived in America, the next phase of our immigration would already be underway. Before the year was out, Fariid, Salaam, Moni (who still counted as our dependent), and I would all be US green-card holders. I thanked God. I knew so many like us would never have such an opportunity.

In the time we had left in Beirut, I began the process of packing, sorting through the material remains of nearly two decades worth of life lived in this apartment, in this city I thought would, finally, be my home. But it was not to be. God's providence is greater than what we can know. And once again, violence and conflict were forcing us out of our home, out of the beautiful lives we had so painstakingly built out of our hardships.

I have never taken well to change, to upheaval, and so I was anxious and uncertain in those final days in Beirut. But I was excited, too. I was going to the United States.

America was our last haven. After Palestine, and Syria, and Lebanon, we came to America finally for security. We ran away from wars and conflict and feelings of restlessness and uncertainty. And America was the haven we came to. It had always been my dream to come to the States and to live here, because at my American school in Palestine, they had always spoken to us about the United States, and I wanted to see what they spoke to us about firsthand, not just read about it.

When we came to America, the first thing I thought was, "This land is so spacious." There was space everywhere. Wide open spaces everywhere I looked. Space enough for us. And we didn't even have culture shock, because we had always wanted to come; we had read all their magazines, knew all their ways, from as long ago as when we lived in Damascus. And we spoke the language; we were schooled in English, and we knew the language as well as we knew Arabic, even better than some of the Americans themselves. And I was so excited and so happy to come and live in the States and get rid of insecurity and instability. There, in the Arab world, there was no freedom. No freedom at all. Not like in the States. There, in Beirut, even if we were wearing a cross on our necks, we would have to hide it in our clothes so that nobody knew. So it was like we came to heaven when we came to the States. We were finally free.

My happiest day was when we became citizens, many years after we got our green cards. We had settled down by then, in Houston, near most of my sisters and my brother Sami. And the day we got our passports, we threw a big party at our church so that all our friends and family could come celebrate with us. The day we became citizens, there was a ceremony in a big stadium downtown, and they had a woman speaker there who told us we were becoming a part of the melting pot of America. And then we recited the pledge of allegiance, and we sang the anthem. We should always pledge allegiance to this country. It is the land of plenty, the land of choices. And all during that ceremony, I had tears in my eyes and goose bumps — the whole time. It was the wish of my heart to be an American. My prayers had been answered. I thank God always for this country; may God protect this country that accepted us and adopted us, for where else would we go? As Palestinian Christians, no one else accepted us. No one wanted us. So America became our homeland, and I pray to God, "Please, God, please, God, keep this country the land of plenty." This, finally, is where we belonged. This country is our home.

LEYLA · THE DARK, BEAUTIFUL NIGHT

Houston, 2002

In 1948, my grandmother, four months into her marriage to my grandfather, fled Haifa, Palestine, where both of them had grown up and where they had made their new home together. On the day they left, mere weeks before the *nakba*, my grandparents had hoped to be able to return to their home after the violence calmed down, but of course, they never did. No one in our family has ever been back to the home my grandparents left behind in 1948.

And Grandma told me once that in that moment, she was filled with such depth of fear and loss and anxiety that it was all she could do to hold on to her new husband's hand for dear life as they boarded the crowded ship that would take them to Beirut. She was four months pregnant with my mother. Grandma says that her faith then was nothing compared to what it became — that she did not trust in God as she should have. Still, I imagine that the only thing that brought her and Grandpa through that moment was the strong Christian faith that I always knew in them.

For many recent decades, scientists believed that a woman is born with all the egg cells she will ever have in her lifetime already within her reproductive organs. If so, then when my grandmother fled Haifa in 1948, with the forming body of my mother inside her womb, then the beginnings of my own self, my own identity were caught up in that moment, too. I can see myself, the future daughter of the baby who grew in my grandmother's belly, nestled within that very baby, itself nestled within her mother, like a living set of Russian dolls. I imagine that the loss and fear of that moment somehow seeped into me, and I have been holding it in the core of my being ever since, like my own egg. And that if you break that egg open, there's this even more hidden part, golden and warm. And that is my faith. It is the faith of my mother and grandmother, and it is the thing that carried us all, one inside the other, through that awful moment, and will carry us through the rest, too.

More recent research suggests that women likely produce new egg cells throughout their reproductive years, which is good news for those who struggle with infertility. But whatever the latest science says about the biological processes of fertility, we are all products of our ancestors; each of us is the smallest (so far) in our own series of Russian dolls, nestled within others, through whom and by whom we have received the gifts of identity.

Of course, we have to be made aware of these gifts; our eyes have to be opened to them for the abundance of their blessings to be revealed to us. And that wasn't always the case for me. As a very pale-skinned girl growing up in the suburbs of Houston, I had no idea of the richness of my ancestry.

I remember with searing clarity the first time I learned my own identity.

I must have been fourteen or fifteen years old. I was a freshman in high school, and one day in our social-studies class, we finished up a unit about World War II and the Holocaust with a screening of some film about Anne Frank. The last scene in the movie was one of Anne Frank's father, who had survived the concentration camp and returned to a new kind of life. In the scene, he stands before a storefront window with a number of televisions all tuned to a news station. The news headline being broadcast is of the creation of the nation-state of Israel, and the implication (as I understood it at the time) was that, in this event, there was some offer of hope or redemption from the horrors that Mr. Frank had suffered at the hands of Nazi brutality.

After school, I met my older sister on the bench outside the band hall where we always waited for my mom to pick us up. The film I had watched earlier in the day must have made an impression, because I started telling Zeyna about it as we sat side by side:

"In the end, though, the Jews got their own homeland!" I told her excitedly. "Isn't that great?"

Zeyna turned to me with wide eyes and raised her pointer finger at me in the mode of instruction. She spoke slowly and seriously: "Don't you dare say that to Mom when she gets here."

I don't remember what happened after that moment. I imagine that Zeyna must have told me something like, *Um, hello? WE ARE PALESTINIAN!* I think she had to have given me the briefest of history and identity lessons in the few minutes before Mom's Buick arrived. But beyond that moment of horror on Zeyna's face, I have no memory.

Thinking back, I don't remember hearing — much less using — the words "Palestine" or "Palestinian" in my early childhood at all. We rarely talked about Arabs even. "Arabic" was definitely part of my lingo, and I knew that was what my mom and her family spoke. And we have always been especially close (both emotionally and geographically) to my grandparents and the large and loving web of great-aunts, my great-uncle, and their spouses and children and grandchildren that I grew up around, the extended family that helped to raise me.

But I didn't know that this family made me different from my peers in any way. I just assumed that everyone had a mom who spoke a second language. I thought everyone saw dozens of cousins and extended family members for a couple of hours on a weekly basis every Sunday after church. It never occurred to me that other people didn't celebrate major holidays with more than a hundred relatives.

The first time I ever questioned those assumptions was one Sunday maybe a year or so after the incident with my sister. Zeyna had invited a friend of hers — I think her name was Mary — to church with us that day. And since our extended-family gathering for "coffee" at one of my great-aunts' houses afterward was a foregone conclusion to our Sunday morning routine, Mary came with us to that, too.

About an hour into it all, we found Mary sitting apart from the rest of us, weeping. If you want to get the attention of a bunch of Arab mothers, sit by yourself and cry. All the aunties came running: "What's wrong? *Habiibti*, are you okay? What's the matter?" they asked.

When she could find space to answer, poor Mary wailed: "I didn't know families could be like this. . . . My family doesn't even get together like this on Thanksgiving! I wish I had a family like yours!"

The existential revelation provided to me by my sister on that day after school, combined with my surprise over Mary's emotional response to my family's usual get-together, inspired the beginnings of a deep dive into my own identity. In my final years of high school, I began to ask questions, to listen to my grandmother's and my aunties' stories, to retain what I heard, as my grandmother had done before me, her whole life. Frustrated by an inability to hear my elders' experiences in their native tongue, I studied Arabic in college, taking both semesters — the full extent of courses for the language that my university offered. And in the waning weeks of my last year, with a teaching job secured for the coming fall and a blissfully empty summer before me to fill as I pleased, I called my grandmother and asked her a question:

"Would it be okay with you if we spent some time together this summer?"

"Yes, of course, *habiibti*," she replied. "I'd love to see you as often as you can come."

"But I mean a *lot* of time, Grandma," I clarified. "I'd like you to tell me about your life, about growing up in Palestine and fleeing in '48 and living in Damascus and Beirut and all that stuff. I was thinking I might get one of those little mini tape recorders, and we could talk all morning every day — for as long as it takes — and I would record it all and keep it. And maybe, someday, I might write it all down."

She was enthusiastic. "Yes, *habiibti*. Yes, Leylati. That's a very nice idea. It would be my pleasure."

And so, here we are, Grandma and me. She sits in her favorite chair in her living room, and I am at one end of the sofa beside her, steaming cups of tea on the side table between us. On my lap is a legal pad of yellow paper that my grandmother found for me among the few remaining items of the printing and stationery shop my grandfather owned until his death two years ago. The mini cassette player in my hand I bought with my own money just last week.

With a bit of a sheepish grin, I press record on the little device and set it down on the table next to my tea. Grandma and I look at each other, and we both start to laugh. I have always loved her laughter. It bubbles up from within her chest, perhaps even from below, from her belly, where her joy lies, where her faith lies, where once even I lay — or at least one half of me — a tiny, microscopic egg within my mother's womb as she was carried safely within *her* mother's womb that day, more than fifty years ago, through trauma and tragedy.

And here we are now, to remember it all together. To keep it for my own children some day, and for their children, too. To retain it.

And so we begin. We start with laughing now.

LEYLA · THE DARK, BEAUTIFUL NIGHT

Austin, Texas, February 11, 2024

I look white. I've got fair skin and hazel-green eyes, like my grandmother's, and light brown hair. My dad, *Allah yerhamhu*, used to say I have the map of Ireland stamped on my face (my father being half Irish, half Croatian). But only when you look casually, I think. Look a little further, at my deep-set eyes, at the bones of my face, at the fullness of my calves and thighs, and you'll see that I am Palestinian.

Still, the world doesn't look so closely. The world glances at the most superficial aspects of our appearances and makes all sorts of assumptions. So as I was growing up — and still to this day — the world experiences me as *white*. Which means, of course, that I experience the world as a white person, and until I was nearly an adult, never questioned that experience.

So while my sister, with her light brown skin that turned almost black in that Texas summer sun, must have grown up experiencing herself as somehow different, as decentered, as non-white, I always experienced the world only with the privilege that whiteness brings. Which must be why Zeyna knew she was Palestinian well before I did. Which is why she was in a position to enlighten and educate me all those years ago. Which is why she maybe has never had to work out her own identity as I have done, grappling with the implications of a family history that doesn't match the color of my skin, and learning to stand up for my own people in an American society that sees Palestinians as the enemy.

Once, I read Layla Saad's *Me and White Supremacy* with a small group of white women. Only about halfway through the book, as I heard the stories of the other women's experiences with it, which felt strikingly and weirdly different from mine, did I realize that Saad's "important note" to "biracial, multiracial and People of Color" near the beginning of the text was actually meant for me.

"Important note for biracial, multiracial, and People of Color who hold white privilege," Saad writes. She continues, "This work is for you too. However, your experience of doing this work will be very different from the experiences of white people who are not biracial, multiracial, or People of Color. While you receive the benefits of white privilege from being lighter skinned or white passing, that does not mean you have had the same experiences as a white person. . . . Your white privilege does not erase or minimize your other identities or experiences."

While I receive the benefits of white privilege, I am not a white person. I have not had the same experiences as a white person. I am mixed-race: one-half Palestinian, one-quarter Irish, and one-quarter Croatian, which makes me a Person of Color. It has taken me a very long time to realize that. I am still on that journey.

My grandmother dreamed of coming to America almost her whole life. From the time she was a small child at an American Quaker boarding school, she admired so much about Americans and America, about the ways of the West. And when she finally got here, to her beloved States, and found her belonging, it was like a miracle. She thanked God every day, every moment, it seemed, for this country. "The land that I love," she called it.

And America was a haven — *is* a haven — for my Palestinian family. My great-aunts — Rose, Abla, Nuha, Samira, Laila, Inaam, and Elham — and my great-uncle Sami, my grandparents, my uncle Moni, my aunt Salaam, my own mom, my many cousins and second cousins and their children. They all found refuge and belonging here. We are Americans.

But being Palestinian-American has seemed to only get harder as the decades go on. Our *whiteness* is liminal, limited. So many of my darker-skinned relatives have experienced racism head-on. My sister. My first cousin Joseph, Moni's son. Or the older generations whose English still carries an accent. The lilt to my mother's voice that is so dear to me signals she is *other* to the white folks she encounters every day.

And my fair skin has not immunized me from this country's racism. My privilege has placed me in the position of overhearing the hatred many in this country have for my people and finding the courage to confront it. I have had to grapple with the work of correcting their stereotypes and outing myself as Palestinian. I lost a job I wanted because, in telling the story of my faith, I shared the story of my grandmother and was therefore deemed a poor fit compared to the white man who was hired.

America was a kind of salvation for my grandmother. And I thank God for the providence that brought her here. But it has been a mixed blessing for me. This is the legacy that we leave for my own children, and the ones that come after them.

My daughter Beatrice is even lighter-skinned than I am, though I didn't think it was possible. Her white-blond hair grew out into lovely bouncy curls when she was very young. It has settled into waves with darker streaks that I brush and braid for her at night before she goes to bed. In many ways, she looks like Ben's family — a little mirror-image of her English *paternal* grandmother. But I see glimpses of myself, of Mom, of Grandma in her still now and then. In the thickness of that long braid. In the strength of her emotions, which she has not yet learned — which I hope she will never learn — to keep hidden within. In the sound of her laugh. The way it bubbles up from deep inside of her, down in her belly, where even now, perhaps, she carries the egg of yet another generation. Another daughter of Palestine to make her way in this wide world.

Leyla. It is my name. It is the word that contains my identity. In Arabic, spelled slightly differently from the name, the word means, plainly, "night." Turned into a name, it gains meaning both in the identity it attains and in the layers of poetic imagery it accrues: it is a very fine wine, the poet's idealized woman, the beauty of a dark, dark night. It is ironically fitting that I, such a light-skinned daughter of my family, have been named after the dark, beautiful night. I thank my lucky stars.

الحمد لله
Praise be to God.

ACKNOWLEDGMENTS

I have been carrying my grandmother's stories in my body for more than two decades. They have never been a burden, but ever since that summer when I interviewed her, they have been quickening within me, and I have longed to deliver them safely into the world. It has taken a long, long time, and it would never have happened without the help and support of so many people.

My first debt of gratitude is, of course, to my grandmother, Bahi Oueida, may she rest in peace, whose ability to "retain," to use her word, was impressive. I am honored and amazed that she entrusted her stories to me. I pray I have stewarded them well.

And I must acknowledge, too, the support of my father, Joe Kamalick, whose love for me I can still feel even from the grave. And my adoptive grandmother and one-time mentor, Nardi Reeder Campion, whose encouragement from beyond this life I literally experienced through numerous notes she had left written down for me on my first initial attempts to begin to tell Bahi's story many years ago. The faith that these dear ones had in me as a writer and storyteller when they lived powered my confidence to finally write this book.

Moving back into the land of the living, it is imperative that I thank my mother, May Kamalick, who has always loved and supported me with the kind of fierceness only a mother can have. Waiting on the sidelines for these stories — which are also her stories — to be brought forth was impossibly hard for her but much appreciated by me. And I give thanks for the whole extended family that is my mother's gift to me: the people who grew up alongside me and the ones who helped to raise me. These are also their stories, at least in parts. I hope my telling has given insight and honor to their ancestors, too, and done no harm.

I am grateful for a number of others whose work and advice have helped midwife these stories into existence: Romulus Stefanut, theology librarian at the University of the South, digitized the audio tapes of the hours upon hours of recorded interviews with my grandmother, making them accessible to and easily navigated by me when I finally sat down to write. My auntie Lena Habiby filled in a number of gaps that were missing in my *Khalo* Sami's narrative.

The immediate interest that Angela Yarber of Tehom Center Publishing expressed in this book's potential and the space she created for me in her NaNoWriMo 2023 cohort finally lit the spark I needed to get these stories out. My friend, colleague, and fellow Middle Easterner Julie Hoplamazian provided encouragement and such helpful conversation all along the way. And the support of Nicole Janelle, Rachel Kessler, and Lauren Grubaugh Thomas, who founded Palestinian Anglicans & Clergy Allies with me, was equally sustaining. Ali Tamutus helped get the manuscript across the finish line to publication. And Elizabeth Fellicetti, my small-church friend, shepherded me through my first baby steps into the industry of authorship mere months before her tragic death; her generous wisdom- and knowledge-sharing and her beautiful spirit were great gifts to me.

A very special thanks goes to Megan Greene Roberts, whose writer's eye and brilliant advice were always my go-to when I had questions or concerns about the craft and process of writing a book. And her first read of my manuscript was instrumental in bringing it to its completion.

And, of course, many thanks to my Eerdmans editor, Lisa Ann Cockrel, whose kind words about the draft that appeared in her inbox made me feel like a true author. I lucked out landing such a talented editor and guide for my experience of publishing these precious stories.

Finally, my deepest gratitude and love goes to my family: my children, Fred, Beatrice, and Toby, are the source of my happiness, the daily reminder of God's many blessings, and the inheritors of the legacy my grandmother left to me. And there are no words to express my thanksgiving for my husband, Ben. Aside from the real work he did in reading the manuscript and providing his input, his love, support, and partnership are the rock on which everything else stands. This book is dedicated to my grandmother and my father, but it exists only because of Ben.

And one more acknowledgment is necessary: I must acknowledge the suffering of my fellow Palestinians — from my great-grandparents' generation until today, in present-day Palestine/Israel and in the diaspora. The oppression, persecution, discrimination, and injustice that they, we, and you all have faced and continue to face with faith and fortitude simultaneously breaks and fills my heart. It was the threat of genocide to my people in Gaza (hopefully never to succeed) in the weeks and months following October 7, 2023, that finally inspired me to tell my grandmother's stories to the world so that her truth, my truth, our truth, God willing, might help to set us free.

For discussion questions and a photo gallery for *Daughters of Palestine*, visit https://thankfulpriest.com/daughters-of-palestine/.